Lamps & Other Lighting Devices, 1850-1906

Distributed by Charles Scribner's Sons, New York

Lamps
&
Other Lighting Devices
1850-1906

Solar lamps; gas chandeliers, brackets and fixtures;
brass mechanical kerosene lamps, chandeliers and lanterns; student
lamps; glass kerosene banquet, stand, hand and footed hand
lamps; fonts, globes and chimneys; fancy decorated
glass vase ("Gone With the Wind") lamps

Archer & Warner, 1850
Cornelius & Sons, c. 1875
Hitchcock Lamp Co., 1887
King Glass Co., c. 1890
Bellaire Goblet Co., 1891
Macbeth-Evans Glass Co., c. 1900
Fostoria Glass Co., 1906

Compiled by the Editors of The Pyne Press

AMERICAN HISTORICAL CATALOG COLLECTION

THE PYNE PRESS
Princeton

Lamps & Other Lighting Devices, 1850-1906

an historical introduction

The vision of young Abraham Lincoln reading his borrowed books by the light of an open fire is familiar to every American schoolchild. It is an image which reflects harsh reality rather than romance. No matter how attractive firelight may look to modern eyes on a cold evening, it is, at best, an uncertain source of illumination. Yet in early nineteenth-century Kentucky, as in most frontier societies, an open fire was the chief source of artificial light after sundown. Only candles or the crudest of open wick lamps were available to supplement it. They were, in fact, the only means of artificial illumination available even in more sophisticated circles until the end of the eighteenth century. Attempts to improve lighting methods then engaged seekers for new fuels, inventors, mechanics and manufacturers for over a century.

Candles, known since Roman times, have remained popular until the present because of the soft beauty of their light and, as compared to many early illuminating fuels, their relative odorlessness. By the middle of the nineteenth century numerous substances were being used in their manufacture. A pamphlet published as an advertisement in Philadelphia in 1850 describes in detail the various forms of candles and candleholders then available. Entitled "A Familiar Treatise on CANDLES, LAMPS AND GAS LIGHTS; with Incidental Matters Prepared for the Use of their Customers," the pamphlet was published by Archer & Warner, who characterized themselves as "Manufacturers of Gas Fixtures, Chandeliers, Lamps, Girandoles, &c." Like many works originally printed as giveaways, it has become extremely rare.

Its first chapter on candles states:

> Wax and various animal fats and vegetable oils form the constituents of candles. Of these the finest candle is produced by wax, the natural color of which is pure white, though from a mixture of honey and bee-bread, it comes from the hive of a dark yellow color, and has to be bleached by exposure in thin plates to the action of light and air. . . . It is frequently adulterated with resin, suet, white lead, potato starch and spermaceti. . . .
>
> Spermaceti is found in the form of a spongy, oily mass, in the head of the *Physeter macrocephalus* or cachelot, a species

of whale. The fore part of the skull has a large triangular cavity ten or twelve feet long and four or five feet deep, which contains nearly a ton of crude spermaceti. It is in a fluid state, and a hole being made in the upper part of the head of the dead whale, the substance is lifted out by means of buckets. When it cools it becomes of the consistence of fat. It is pressed in bags and suffered to drip. What escapes is known as sperm oil. The remainder is refined, in the manufactories, after it is brought home, by means of pressure, boiling in water, and mixture with a weak lye of potash. The mass thus obtained is white, flaky and crystalline, as it is found in the shops. When pure it has very little taste or smell, has a high lustre, and is exceedingly translucent. A small quantity of spermaceti is found in other whales, and in the fat of all fish. It melts at 112 degrees, and requires 133 degrees for its combustion.

Stearine or stearic acid, of late years, has been much used in the manufacture of candles. Tallow is composed of three substances called by chemists stearin, margarin and olein. . . . The solid substance, after being deprived of the margarin, is run into candles, and sold under the names of "star" candles, "adamantine" candles, &c. In the West, where large numbers of hogs are slaughtered annually, this manufacture is carried on to a great extent, and the olein resulting from it, is known in commerce as "Lard Oil." Of this we shall have more to say in its proper place.

Tallow is usually obtained from beef and mutton suet, though it can be had, of various qualities, from all animals, and even from the human body. It is melted and purified, and then either run into moulds or "dipped." The latter give out a very poor light, scarcely enough to "make darkness visible" — and are principally used in the country, where oil is not to be had, wax or spermaceti is too dear, and the knowledge of the brilliant light to be obtained from simple lard, through means of our solar lamp, has not yet penetrated.

In addition to describing the most commonly used animal fuels, the "Treatise" alludes to a number of vegetable oils utilized in the manufacture of candles. One of these, derived from the fruit of the candle-berry myrtle, was common in Louisiana and other parts of the South. Some vegetable tallow evidently was imported from the Orient, but, on the whole, Americans utilized animal fats, both for candles and for lamps.

Holders for candles, the "Treatise" makes clear, were available in great variety of design and in a wide price range:

Candlesticks, the use of which is as ancient as that of candles, are made of various shapes and sizes — and of a variety of materials. As we do not manufacture the cheaper kinds, which are made of tin, iron and japanned ware, and may be purchased at any hardware store, we shall merely speak of those of better quality. Ornamented candlesticks or girandoles, for holding any number of candles, from one upward, are now mostly constructed of brass, and silvered, gilded or bronzed. Sometimes they are ornamented with ormulu, and frequently made of Damascus ware, of which our ware-rooms show some splendid specimens. According to the taste and fancy of the purchaser, they can be decorated with cut-glass and other ornaments. We have, however, several hundred different patterns, mostly from original designs by our own artist, and some from the most approved French and English models. Of chandeliers, which are suspended candlesticks, we have a great variety, and are able from the large number of workmen we employ, to manufacture to any pattern selected, at the shortest notice. But lamps, which are so much cheaper, have replaced candles to so great an extent — as gas, wherever it can be had, has replaced oil, that the manufacture of girandoles has become comparatively insignificant. Gas is by far the cheapest and best illuminating substance, and after this, lard and lard oil.

Lamps, indeed, had not simply replaced candles. In their most primitive form they were perhaps even more ancient. Crude lamps made of stone and pottery are among the remains of the ancient civilizations of the Near East. Like the iron Betty lamps of seventeenth-century New England, these early grease lamps are in the form of a shallow saucer, extended to a trough at one or more ends. The saucer was filled with oil; a wick of twisted fiber floated in the oil and was pulled into the trough where it could be lit. These open lamps had several disadvantages. Oil spilled frequently, and because combustion was incomplete, the light flickered and smoked. In Europe vegetable oils, including olive oil, rapeseed oil, and sunflower seed oil, were frequently burned in these lamps. In this country the most common fuels were fish and whale oils. To the other drawbacks of an open lamp these fuels added an unpleasant odor.

By the late eighteenth century the open grease lamp had been replaced almost entirely by various forms of lamps formed of a base, a closed font to hold the fuel and a burner with one or more vertical tubes through which the wick was pulled. These common lamps were made of a variety of materials — glass, tin, pewter, britannia metal, brass and silver. The fuels most generally used in them were described thus in Archer & Warner's "Treatise":

> Of animal oils, the fish oils were first used, and at one time most extensively. They are being rapidly superseded by lard and lard oil. The best of the fish oils, is that from the spermaceti whale, of which we have before spoken. It is of a light lemon color, nearly white, burns with a clear, bright flame, and contains Carbon 79.05; Hydrogen 11.6, Oxygen 8.9. Ordinary fish oils, passed through animal charcoal to purify them, form most of the "Sperm Oil" of commerce.

3

The common whale oil is taken from the whale known among naturalists as *Balaena Mysticetus*, on whose body, the blubber, or fat, from which the oil is rendered, is about six inches in thickness, except on the under lip, where two feet depth is found. The quantity yielded by a single whale varies from one, two to three and even four tons, in weight. The oil itself is of a reddish or yellowish color, and burns with a rather unpleasant smell. It may be burned without odor, and with quite a brilliant light, in one of our solar lamps, but under ordinary circumstances, it is by no means an agreeable substance, in producing illumination.

Other fish, including the sea-unicorn, porpoise, sword-fish, &c., and various amphibious animals, furnish oil of better or worse quality.

Fish oil may be purified so as to become quite white, though never equal to sperm oil. Most of these processes have been kept secret. One of the best methods, which was first invented and is generally used in this country, is as follows: The oil is first filtered through strainers of linen canvass, suspended by a frame over a large trough. It is then put into immense kettles to be bleached by potash. One hundred pounds, of the best quality of this substance, is dissolved in 15 gallons of pure spring or rain water, and the solution boiled down to 9 gallons. Into a boiler containing 100 gallons of oil, at the temperature of 60 deg. F., 2 gallons of the boiled solution is poured, and the whole mass thoroughly stirred for 15 minutes. Heat is then applied till it is raised to 80 or 90 deg. F., and to prevent setting, the stirring is kept up. When the temperature rises to 90 deg., the fire is extinguished, and the stirring discontinued. In about six hours the whole is found to be white and transparent. In large factories steam is used to regulate the temperature. Sperm oil is also frequently treated in this way, being found to be exceedingly improved by the process.

Lard oil, of which an enormous amount is annually manufactured in this country, and which, as an article of common consumption is continually increasing, is manufactured by various processes, all of a similar character.

Lard oil was produced by boiling lard until the liquid separated from the solid stearin (the latter as has been pointed out then being used for candles). Alcohol was sometimes added to hasten the separation, and small amounts of camphor might be added to improve the odor. During the 1840's and '50's another fuel, consisting of a mixture of turpentine and alcohol was briefly popular. It was sold under the names of camphene, pine oil, or burning fluid. Camphene burned well, but it proved to be highly explosive and frightful accidents resulted from its use. Lamps made to burn camphene may be distinguished by their longer wicks which do not descend below the base plate of the burner. This design was necessary in order to keep any flame as far as possible from the font.

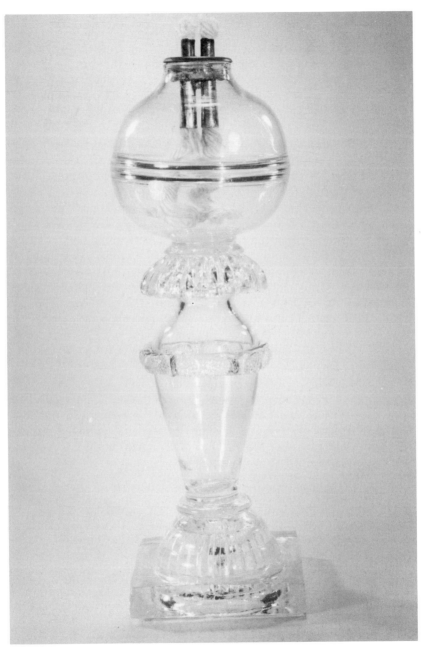

Colorless glass oil lamp with blown font and standard on hand-pressed base. Similar to lamps attributed to Thomas Cains, working at South Boston Glassworks, 1813-1823. *Old Sturbridge Village.*

Although fluid oil lamps, especially the glass ones, were often elaborately made, the principle on which they operated was simple. The oil rose through the wick by capillary action and was consumed, not without a certain amount of smoke and odor. In the early nineteenth century the burner was often set in a round of cork which was pressed into an opening in the top of the font. By about 1830 threaded burners were being produced. They screwed into a pewter collar glued to the font.

While these common lamps were certainly far more satisfactory aesthetically and practically than the Bettys and crusies that had preceded them, and more economical than candles, efforts were made continuously to improve the quality of artificial illumination. A major breakthrough was made in 1783 when a Swiss, Ami Argand, perfected a new form of burner. The Argand burner employed a cylindrical wick, mounted between two metal tubes. Holes or slots at the bottom of the burner admitted air from below. This provided a draft of air within the wick as well as on the outside. The efficiency of the Argand lamp was further improved by use of a tall cylindrical chimney. Because of the completeness of combustion produced by increased draft, Argand lamps provided far more light with less smoke than common lamps. With those who could afford the best, Argand lamps were an immediate success. George Washington equipped Mount Vernon with Argands fashioned of Sheffield plate.

Argands had only one disadvantage. To maintain a consistent flow of fuel the reservoir was placed above the burner, feeding fuel by gravity. The reservoir in this position cast a shadow on the area lighted. Over the next several decades various adaptations of the Argand lamp were introduced in an effort to minimize the shadow. Several of them are mentioned by Archer & Warner:

> Other lamps have been introduced from time to time, under the names of the "Annular," "Parker's Sinumbra," "Quarrel's Sinumbra," "Quarrel's Albion," "Isis," "Parker's Hot Oil," "Keir's Fountain," "Parker's Fountain," and the "Carcel" lamps. Some of these are curious—the Carcel especially, which is a mechanical lamp of much merit, but is so liable to get into disorder, that it never has been able to work its way into general use. Our solar lard lamp has supplanted all these, being simple and practical, and giving a brilliant light, while it burns any description of fats and any coarse oil, without either smoke or smell.

These were for the most part various forms of astral lamps in which the reservoir was made in the form of a narrow ring, placed below the burner and feeding fuel to it through slender tubes. In sinumbra lamps (from the Latin "sine umbra"—without shadow) the ring was

6

oval in cross-section, thus permitting more light to penetrate downwards from the burner. Most of these lamps were rather tall, since the light was intended to fall from above.

The Carcel lamp referred to above was developed in 1798 to burn fairly viscous oils. Spring-operated pumps maintained the flow of oil to the wick. Since the flow was steady, so was the light, but the mechanism was a delicate one, as the "Treatise" points out, and the lamp was therefore unreliable. The solar lamp, which came into fairly common use at mid-century, used a deflector shaped like an inverted saucer to direct an external draft against the flame of an Argand burner. It produced an intense white light and, since it also directed heat downward towards the reservoir, could be used with lard and other heavy fuels.

Whether in the form of solar lamps, common oil lamps, or the elaborate branched candleholders known as girandoles, the most fashionable lighting devices of the mid-nineteenth century were made of a composite of materials. A marble plinth held a shaft of brass or other metal, often richly finished. The font of an oil lamp or the globe of a solar lamp would be made of glass, sometimes decoratively cut or engraved. Cut glass prisms were often used to enhance the glitter of both candles and lamplight.

The manufacture of such lighting devices was an elaborate process. A visitor to the fireproof factory of Cornelius of Philadelphia, then the country's foremost producer of lighting devices, described the various steps used in producing fine fixtures in 1860. The first step was the creation of a model in wax. From this model a mold was cast by the lost wax process. The details of the resulting mold were then deepened and refined by hand chasing with steel tools. From this mold, a brass master pattern was made. Often curved portions of the pattern were then flattened, since it was easier to cast flat surfaces. Later, the resulting castings would be re-shaped by hammering with wooden mallets to give the piece the desired rounded shapes. Finished patterns were sent to the casting room where the actual process of manufacturing a lamp began.

> Each caster works at a wooden trough about eight feet long, thirty inches wide, and twenty inches deep. Into this trough he carefully sieves prepared sand, slightly moistened. His first step is to place across the trough a planed board, about two feet long and sixteen inches wide. Upon this an iron frame, being one half of what is technically called a "flask," is placed. This frame has a depth of about two and a half inches. Within this, and upon the board, are arranged the brass patterns to be reproduced. Upon these is dusted, or sieved, a coating of fine facing-sand. The frame is then rapidly filled up from the trough. By a light

bound the workman springs from the ground upon the sand, which he thus presses compactly into the frame until a solid mass is formed. The top is then smoothed off, and a board, similar to the lower one, is placed upon it, and the frame is reversed. The board that had been the lower one is removed, revealing the pattern imbedded in the sand. The other section of the frame or flask is fitted in its place, and filled up as its fellow. The two are then separated, the patterns are carefully removed, and grooves or gates are made in the sand. The flasks are then re-united and firmly fastened together by means of screws or clamps, and ranged along with the open side upward. We are careful now to keep to the windward of the furnaces, while the caster by means of long tongs, takes out a crucible of molten brass and pours the fiery liquid into the "gates" which lead into the mould. A few minutes are sufficient to chill the metal in the "flask;" the clamps are removed, and the sand is shaken out. The casting is found complete, with the exception of some fragments of brass which cling around the edges. It is a matter of surprise to see how faithfully the finest chased work has been transferred from the original pattern to the copy. . . .

There is no difficulty experienced in finding the whereabouts of the filing-room. The incessant grating of scores of files creates a din that would guide a blind man to the spot. Here the castings are conveyed from the foundry. They are first "edged up" with coarse rasps, and then finished smoothly with finer tools. In many instances a number of castings have to be joined together to form one piece. When this is the case, the several component parts are conveyed to the soldering-room, where they are carefully fitted together, taking care to leave one edge more prominent than the other, the sections are then put into their proper places, and retained there by wrapping them with iron wire. Particles of brass solder, which looks like brazen saw-dust, are mingled with water and nicely applied along the projecting edge of the section. The entire piece is then placed in a furnace where the solder is melted. The work has, of course, to go through another filing after that process is finished. The joints must be made with a great deal of care, or in gas fixtures the subtle fluid would make its escape through any tiny opening left by the workman.

Before the castings leave the filing and soldering-rooms, there is frequently much to be done in the way of turning and twisting of branches, crumpling of leaves, drilling holes, &c., &c. The articles are then sent to the dipping rooms, whither we will now wend our way.

When the brass comes out of the hands of the filers, it is dirty and discolored, and has more or less sand, or other foreign matter clinging to it. The first act of the dipper is to take hold of the brazen article with a pair of tongs and dip it into a jar of acid; a moment only is required by this process to remove every particle of dirt and soil from the surface; the hungry chemical

8

eats it off, and would soon devour the brass itself if sufficient time was given it. The dipper will not suffer that, though, and he speedily takes out the cleansed metal and places it into water, which forthwith washes off the acid and puts a stop to its ravages. The first operation is called "pickling." The color is then essentially brass-like, as the "pickle" has devoured every extraneous substance from the surface. The article (say a girandole) which is undergoing the cleansing process then is dipped into another jar, the contents of which are a mystery to us. This has the effect to render the surface a rich sulphur color. This operation occupies but a moment; the girandole is again washed in clean water, and then plunged into a chemical combination called an ormolu; in a few minutes the color of the metal is changed to a dirty yellow. The ormolu is then washed off, and the surface of the girandole is found, upon close inspection, to have been eaten into minute molecules by the ravenous ormolu. One more dip into an acid which makes the brass a rich, pale gold color, finishes the chemical ordeal. After the girandole is cleansed in water, it presents a rich and uniform though dull gold color. This dulness forms a good foil, and contrasts handsomely with the prominent parts of the design, which are afterwards richly burnished, the ormolu having prepared the surface of the metal for that operation.

At this point in the manufacturing process, the most expensive of bases might be removed to receive an electroplated coating of silver. The greater number of bases and branches for girandoles and gas fixtures, however, proceeded through operations which gave the brass itself a variety of finishes.

There is a little army of hands employed in the burnishing-room. The tools used here are of a great variety of shapes; they are formed either of highly polished steel or a very hard material called bloodstone. The prominent parts of the work are highly polished by means of these burnishing tools, which are dipped freely into a dark colored liquid. Thoughts of deadly poisons again take possession of our mind, but we experience much relief on being assured that the mysterious chemical is nothing more than small beer!—less it could not conveniently be. The parts of the surface of the metal which are not burnished, are left "dead" or "matted," as they came from the ormolu. Burnishing is an important process. Much of the beauty and character of the work depends upon a judicious selection of the parts to be brought out by the burnisher. It is to the proper development of the design, what lights and shades are to a good picture. After the brass is burnished, it is again cleansed by means of acids, and finally washed in hot water, the heat of which soon causes the work to dry: it is then thrown into a trough containing bookbinder's paper-shavings, which completes the drying. The work is now ready for lacquering. . . .

One of a pair of bronze Argand lamps with etched glass shades. Manufactured in England for sale by Alfred Wells of Boston, c. 1830. *Old Sturbridge Village*.

Astral lamp with marble base, brass and cut glass shaft and frosted and clear glass shade. Imported, probably from England, by Clark & Coits, New York City, c. 1840. *Old Sturbridge Village*.

The lacquering room is a very uncomfortable place in hot weather, being liberally supplied with stoves, which are kept constantly heated. Here the various pieces are taken from their paper bed and placed upon the hot iron, after being carefully brushed. When heated to a certain degree, the articles are taken (by means of proper instruments) to a table, where the lacquer is applied with flat brushes made of camel's hair. The lacquer is composed of a certain gum dissolved in alcohol. Some articles are dipped into the lacquer, and "slung" backwards and forwards to insure its being properly spread over their surface. The lacquering is of the utmost importance, and requires the lacquer to be scientifically made and skillfully applied, to ensure a rich and lasting gold color, unaffected by the action of the atmosphere.

The different parts and ornaments are now ready to be placed in the hands of the fitter, or finisher, and are therefore selected and carried to the respective places arranged for putting them together. One room is occupied entirely by a number of men who are constantly employed in fitting together such gas work as chandeliers, pendants, brackets, &c.; another to girandoles and candelabras; and a third to the numerous class of solar lamps designed for standing upon the table, or for being suspended from the ceiling or against the wall. From all these apartments the goods are taken to meet once more in the packing-room previous to bidding a final farewell to their birth-place.

Some of the ornamental work is painted in particolors to please fanciful tastes; some is bronzed with different shades; while other work is covered with a coating of fine gold, or tastefully enameled. . . .

There are rooms appropriated to the workers in artistic bronze, others occupied by those who are employed at "damask" work. The "damask" is done with lacquer and acids. The candelabras, girandoles, standing solar lamps, and many other articles, are made with a marble base. There is a shop where a number of men are employed cutting and polishing the marble for this branch. We must inspect the enameling on glass, as the operation is exceedingly curious and tasteful. The operator here is an artist. He first makes a sketch on drawing paper, of the design he intends enameling. The glass on which the painting is to be made, is then laid flat upon the drawing. The artist then paints the outlines on the back of the glass. The view to be transferred is perhaps a moonlight scene, with a castle and a bridge, and other pretty etceteras. A piece of stout paper is fitted to the shape of the glass; on this, bits of mother-of-pearl are affixed here and there. The artist puts a small piece on the spot where the moon will come on the picture; another, and a larger piece is placed opposite the bridge, and a still larger portion where it will represent the castle. The artist then paints the glass around these objects, to suit his taste, taking care that the colors shall be opaque. The glass, within the space allotted for the bridge and the castle, is shaded, and the necessary windows, &c., are painted there in outline. A clean circular space is left on the glass for the moon. After the painting is finished, the glass is secured to the paper back on which the bits of pearl have been attached, and an exquisite picture, with the most conspicuous objects in mother-of-pearl, produced. One of these enameled views is put into a handsome brass frame, and forms the centre of a girandole, or a bracket, which would do no discredit to the most elegant drawingroom. . . .

There are other rooms appropriated to glass cutting, grinding and polishing, which are done entirely by steam.

In addition to making girandoles and lamps, Cornelius, Archer & Warner and other firms in Boston, New York and Philadelphia were, by the mid-nineteenth century, producing chandeliers, brackets and other fixtures designed to burn illuminating gas. The use of gas as an illuminant had been known, at least theoretically, since the late seventeenth century. Its first practical application, however, seems not to have occurred until 1792, when an English engineer named Murdock used gas to light his own home. Six years later, he perfected a gas generating apparatus which was used to illuminate an entire factory. In 1812 a company was chartered to supply the city of London with gas. Four years later the interior of Philadelphia's New Theater was illuminated with gas, although a gasworks capable of supplying the general needs of the city was not constructed until 1836. By that time, Baltimore, New York and Boston had already been supplied with gas. By mid-century most major American cities and numerous smaller towns and villages had their own gasworks.

Many of the fixtures designed for use with gas were extremely simple, although the flame itself was often shielded by an elaborately cut or colored glass bowl. Others, like those illustrated in the Archer and Warner "Treatise" of 1850 or the Cornelius catalog of the 1870's reproduced in the following pages, were produced in elaborate forms. The manufacture of the fixtures themselves was a fairly simple process, but involved great precision to avoid any possibility of fatal leakage. According to the pamphlet describing their factory released by Cornelius in 1860:

The manufacture of gas burners is an important feature. These articles are exposed to a great heat when in use, and consequently have to be made of hard cast-iron. The burner is moulded in a solid form; from the caster it goes into the hands of the filer, who "roughs" it off. The next operation is to drill it, to make it hollow. This we fancied must be a very tedious and toilsome task, but we were pleasantly surprised to see the drill scoop out the hard iron with the same facility as if it had been rich old cheese. The turning lathe and the finely tempered drills made nothing of this operation, but chipped out the hard cast-iron as though the employment was rather agreeable than otherwise. The burner has then to go into the hands of the turner, who quickly removes the superfluous iron from the outside, and generally puts a tasty finish upon the article. The burner now looks like an iron ferrule. Before it can be made available for its legitimate use, it must be "tapped" so as to screw on the brass fixtures. It has also to be drilled with two tiny holes, if intended for a "fish-tail" burner, or have a fine slit sawed in the end if designed for a "bat-wing." Both these operations require great skill and caution in the workman. The burner, after this has been performed, is to be polished, and it is then ready for use. . . . We enter one apartment in which great numbers of men are employed in making the keys or faucets of the gas fixtures. They must be made to operate with safety and certainty. This work requires a great deal of care, as an aperture the size of a pin's point would be considered a serious leak. To insure a close fit, each key and its appropriate socket is ground out with emery.

Gas was certainly the most satisfactory illuminant available in the mid-nineteenth century. Archer & Warner detailed some of its advantages:

The advantage of gas-lights is manifest. It is much cheaper, compared with the light it affords, than any other. It saves a deal of time and labor, which would otherwise be expended in filling and trimming lamps, cleaning candlesticks and snuffing candles—to say nothing of the constant trouble and anxiety given by these operations, and the spots of grease and oil which follow them. Gaslights are the very perfection of cleanliness. They can be fixed in any situations—and by means of moveable pipes, may be raised, lowered or transferred, according to choice or necessity. The light is agreeable and if properly managed, which management requires no trouble, gives no smoke. In point of cost proportioned to its brilliance, it is nearly one-third that of lard, burned in our solar lamps, and at least one-sixth that of tallow candles.

Yet gas also had its drawbacks. Despite Archer & Warner's claim, it could not be "fixed in any situation," since the fixture needed to be attached to the wall or ceiling through which the gaspipe was run. A gaslight could hardly be moved to the most convenient spot on desk or worktable or at the bedside. Nor was gas available outside the larger cities and towns. In a still predominantly rural America it could not meet the needs of the majority of the population for a reliable, comparatively inexpensive source of light.

A fuel capable of producing such illumination was patented by Abraham Gesner of Williamsburg, N. Y., in 1854. Gesner called his invention, distilled from bituminous coal and oil shale, "kerosene." Because the raw oil was scarce, kerosene was at first an expensive product. When the Pennsylvania Rock Oil Company brought in its first producing well at Titusville, Pennsylvania, in 1859, however, a cheap source for the raw material of kerosene became available. Although its development was inhibited by the Civil War, by the mid-1860's kerosene had revolutionized domestic lighting.

The first lamps made for kerosene differed little from the composite common oil lamps and solar lamps of mid-century. In fact, just as in the twentieth century many nineteenth-century lamps were electrified, so in the 1860's and '70's numerous earlier oil lamps were converted to burn kerosene. The first successful kerosene burner, the "Vienna" burner, was introduced to the United States in 1856. Like the earlier Argand burner, it had vertical slits in the base to admit air. There was a narrow slit in the top to hold a flat wick which could be raised and lowered by a thumb wheel. A simple collar of metal held the lamp chimney in place.

Although these features — the slit to accommodate a flat wick, wick wheels, chimney collar, and perforated base — would characterize all kerosene burners, numerous patents covering various modifications and improvements were issued over the next two decades. George W. Brown, a well-known Connecticut toymaker, was one of the American pioneers in the burner business. Starting with a small shop in Forestville in 1862, he sold his prosperous firm to the Bristol Brass and Clock Co. six years later. He continued his interest in the manufacture of burners and in 1876, 1879 and 1888 patented lamp improvements that were assigned to Bristol Brass. One of the earliest American patents was granted to John J. Marcy of Meriden, Connecticut, in 1863 for a burner which featured a hinged reflector and chimney holder. This permitted easy filling of the reservoir. Marcy's patent was assigned to the firm of Edward Miller, one of the country's leading distributors of lamp burners.

Another important patent was granted to Lewis J. Atwood of the firm of Plume & Atwood in 1873. The firm, founded in 1869, is still in business as a manufacturer of lamp burners. Atwood had previously been foreman of the burner department of Holmes, Booth and Haydens of Waterbury, Connecticut, perhaps the best-known manufacturer of lamp burners. Other important manufacturers were Bristol Brass, Benedict & Burnham, Bridgeport Brass, and Rochester Burner. The names of burner manufacturers and patent dates can usually be found on the thumb wheel that controls the height of the wick.

Kerosene lamps are comparatively difficult to date, since the most common types of glass lamps were made throughout the nineteenth and well into the twentieth century. In fact, glass kerosene lamps are still manufactured today, for use in remote rural and wilderness areas and to supply emergency lighting during power failures.

Nevertheless, certain design tendencies do appear over the course of the second half of the century. During the 1860's the composite lamp, with marble base, metal shaft and glass font, remained popular. These were often made, as they had been since the 1840's, with elaborate fonts of cut or overlay glass. During the early 1860's the slightly elongated font of the whale oil lamp was superseded by the globular font more typical of the kerosene lamp. Toward the middle of the decade the font tended to become somewhat flatter in shape. Nevertheless, no hard and fast rules can be drawn. Lamps of the 1890's, displayed in the King Glass and Bellaire Goblet Company catalogs reproduced in the following pages, echo shapes popular a quarter century earlier.

By the middle of the 1860's lamps made entirely of pressed glass became available and the composite lamp lost its popularity. At the same time lamps made entirely of metal also became fashionable. The student lamp, cantilevered from its stem so that light could be placed directly over a book or work surface, was introduced by Carl A. Kleeman of Erfurt, Prussia, in 1863, but was not widely used in the United States until the 1870's. Mechanical lamps were also introduced in the 1870's. One of the most ingenious of these, produced by the Hitchcock Lamp Company of Watertown, New York, is reproduced in the following pages.

The kerosene lamps of the 1860's and 1870's were relatively plain. The last two decades of the nineteenth century and the first decade of the twentieth century witnessed a trend toward elaboration in the use of colored glass, of etched and cut glass, and of handpainted decoration. Chimneys as well as lamp bases were often decorated. Although floor lamps were uncommon, banquet lamps with tall stems became popular. Set on table or sideboard, these provided general illumination. Another form introduced toward the end of one century and popular into the next was the vase lamp. Often called "Gone With the Wind" lamps because of their anachronistic use in that movie's Civil War-era settings, these lamps featured a highly decorated globular or vase-shaped font on a low metal base with a matching globe. In actuality, the vase was a false font. A metal pot inside held the fuel.

Lamps of the second half of the nineteenth century have not, for the most part, engaged the attention of museums as have those of earlier periods. Nevertheless, private collectors and those seeking attractive accessories for interior decoration have maintained a steady demand for these later lighting devices. Wired for electricity many of them continue to perform their original function, the provision of artificial illumination.

15

Suggestions for further reading

The books and articles listed below are confined to those devoted specifically to lamps and lighting devices. Material on manufacturers of lamp bases will also be found in books on the various substances from which such bases were made — pewter, brass, glass, etc. For the latter, Ruth Webb Lee's books on Sandwich and other nineteenth century glass, and Christian Revi's *American Pressed Glass and Figure Bottles* provide much important information.

ARCHER & WARNER. *A Familiar Treatise on Candles, Lamps and Gas Lights; With Incidental Matters, prepared for the Use of Their Customers.* Philadelphia, 1850.

CORNELIUS & BAKER. *Descriptions of the Establishment of Cornelius & Baker.* Philadelphia, 1860.
   The above are rare pamphlets. They have been quoted extensively in the introduction to this volume.

GOULD, ERNEST C. "The Hitchcock Lamp." *Bulletin of the Jefferson County Historical Society*, Vol. 6, No. 23, pp. 6-11.

HAYWARD, ARTHUR H. *Colonial Lighting.* New York: Dover. Third edition of a classic.
   Mostly on early lamps, but some information on Argands and astrals.

HEBARD, HELEN. *Early Lighting.* Rutland, Vt.: Charles Tuttle, 1964.

HOUGH, WALTER. "Collection of Heating and Lighting Utensils in the United States National Museum." *U.S.N.M. Bulletin 141.* Washington. 1928.

MACBETH-EVANS GLASS COMPANY. *Fifty Years of Glassmaking.* Pittsburgh, 1920.

RUSSELL, LORIS S. *A Heritage of Light: Lamps and Lighting in the Early Canadian Home.* Toronto: University of Toronto Press, 1968.
   Don't let the title fool you. Most of the lighting devices discussed were made in the United States. The best coverage of late-nineteenth century lighting devices, particularly kerosene lamps.

THWING, LEROY. Flickering Flames. Rutland, Vt.: Charles Tuttle, 1957.
   An excellent survey.

WATKINS, C. MALCOLM. "Artificial Lighting in America, 1830-1860." Smithsonian *Report* for 1951, pp. 385-407.

——— "Lighting Devices." *The Concise Encyclopedia of American Antiques*, pp. 355-363. New York: Hawthorn, 1969.

Important Public Collections

Many museums, historical societies, and historic houses open to the public hold and display examples of lamps and lighting devices. The major collections listed below stress examples dated prior to 1850, but may include items of later date.

Museum of History and Technology, United States National Museum, Smithsonian Institution, Washington, D.C.

Greenfield Village and Henry Ford Museum, Dearborn, Mich.

Detroit Historical Museum, Detroit, Mich.

Old Sturbridge Village, Sturbridge, Mass.

Society for the Preservation of New England Antiquities, Boston, Mass.

Archer & Warner, 1850

In 1840 one Ellis Archer listed himself in the Philadelphia City Directory as a merchant. Three years later, Mr. Archer had specialized. The directory listing for 1843 describes him as a dealer in camphene oil and lamps. By 1848 he had formed a partnership with Redwood F. Warner. Archer & Warner engaged in the manufacture of gas fixtures and lamps, many of them from designs on which they held patents. In addition, they were importers of lighting devices from England and France which were displayed, along with their own wares, at their showrooms at 119 Chestnut Street.

By 1857 they had expanded sufficiently to support a manufacturing establishment on Race Street. In 1859 William F. Miskey and William O. B. Merrill joined the company which became known as Archer, Warner, Miskey & Co. By 1860 the senior partners had withdrawn and the successor company was known as Miskey, Merrill & Thackara. By this time the company was applying its skills in metal fabrication not only to lighting devices, but to architectural metalwork. Stair railings cast by them had been installed in the Capitol at Washington. The design featured groups of infants, eagles and serpents, entwined in wreaths of foliage and flowers, comprising, according to a Civil War-era *Guide to Philadelphia and its Manufacturers*, ". . . all the curvilinear forms and intricate traceries which lay the heaviest tax upon the skill of the draughtsman and founder."

The 1850 "Treatise" issued by the firm should, perhaps, be classified as a sales brochure rather than a trade catalog. Only three gas fittings and one design for a solar lamp were illustrated. The solar lamp was shown equipped with a tall chimney and glass globe. This was for general illumination. For close work, reading or sewing, paper shades mounted on wire were also supplied. These were to be substituted for the globe when a light cast down on a work surface was desired.

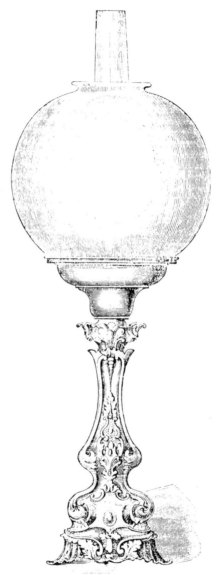

FIG. 4. PATENTED BY ARCHER & WARNER JULY 9, 1850.

Fig. 4. Gas Bracket. Patented by Archer & Warner, March 19, 1850.

Fig. 6. Two-Light Bracket. Patented by Archer & Warner, March 19, 1850.

19

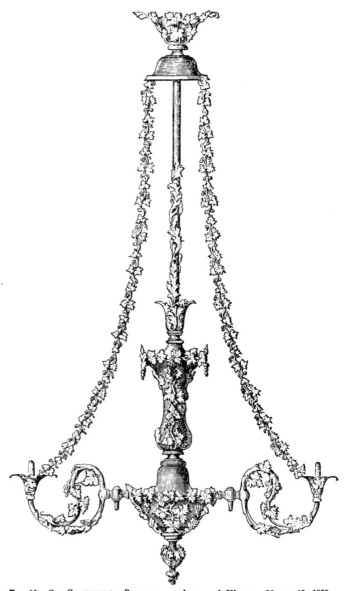

FIG. 10. GAS CHANDELIER. PATENTED BY ARCHER & WARNER, MARCH 19, 1850.

Cornelius & Sons c. 1875

"Mr. Cornelius now makes the most elegant mantel and hanging lamps; his manner of *succeeding* in that, and in *silver plating*, is a *very curious history*, and would deserve to be well told at length." So commented John F. Watson in his *Annals of Philadelphia* in 1857. Unfortunately, neither Mr. Watson nor any of his contemporaries recorded that curious history. All that is known is that one Christian Cornelius came from Amsterdam to Philadelphia in 1783. In 1810 he was listed in the Philadelphia City Directory as a silversmith at the delightful address, 8 Pewterplatter Alley. In 1816 he was listed as a silverplater. By 1825 to the designation of silverplater had been added that of patent lamp manufacturer. In 1833 all mention of silverplating was dropped. Christian Cornelius had founded a dynasty that was to dominate lamp manufacturing in this country by the middle of the nineteenth century.

Over succeeding decades Cornelius' son, son-in-law and, finally, grandsons joined the firm. These changes in ownership were reflected in name changes, listed below according to the dates at which a new name was first used.

> 1840 — Cornelius & Co.
> 1855 — Cornelius, Baker & Co.
> 1860 — Cornelius & Baker
> 1870 — Cornelius & Sons
> 1877 — Cornelius & Co.
> 1886 — Cornelius & Hetherington
> 1888 — Cornelius & Rowland

The firm was dissolved in 1900. As the changes in name occurred with some frequency, it is not difficult to date marked Cornelius lamps with comparative accuracy. Since each manufacturer's castings were unique in detail, unmarked examples can be attributed by careful comparison with marked pieces.

Cornelius achieved nationwide fame. Among their major commissions were the chandeliers for Philadelphia's Academy of Music and most of the gas fixtures for the United States Capitol, including the 2,500 burners used to illuminate the Senate Chamber and the House of Representatives. Cornelius chandeliers and fixtures were also installed in the Capitols of Ohio, Tennessee and other states.

Cornelius' lamps reflected the changing tastes of the nineteenth century. Identified examples from the early 1840's, when the Greek Revival was still at its height, exhibit brass shafts modeled on classical columns. Those of the 1850's reflect the lush and curving naturalistic forms of the then current Rococo Revival. The catalog reproduced in its entirety in the following pages stresses Gothic forms, especially those with the linear Eastlake style of decoration favored in the 1870's.

Only one catalog of this important manufacturer is known to exist in a public collection. All the plates from this copy have been reproduced in the following pages. The catalog is not in perfect condition. The first two pages, in particular, are marred by mildew and foxing; these imperfections have been reproduced as they occur in the original. Certain of the plates in the original catalog are enlivened with gold to indicate the use of gilding. Those shown on pages 41 and 42 of this edition also bear touches of red and blue.

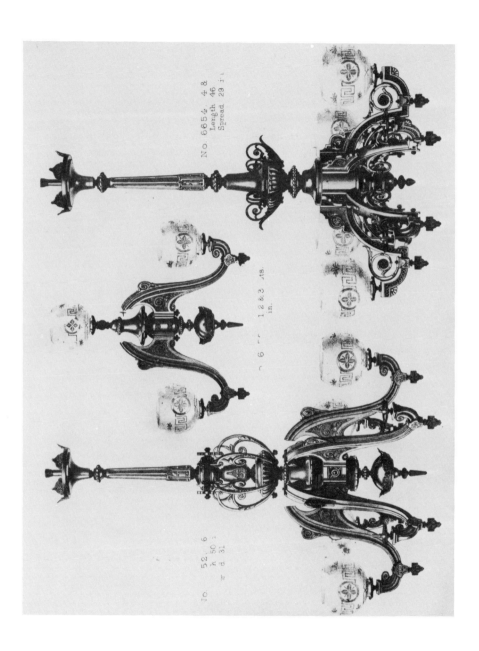

No 6654 4 8
Length 46
Spread 29 in.

No 6 " 1 2 & 3 lts.
in.

No 52 6
h 50 in
d 31

23

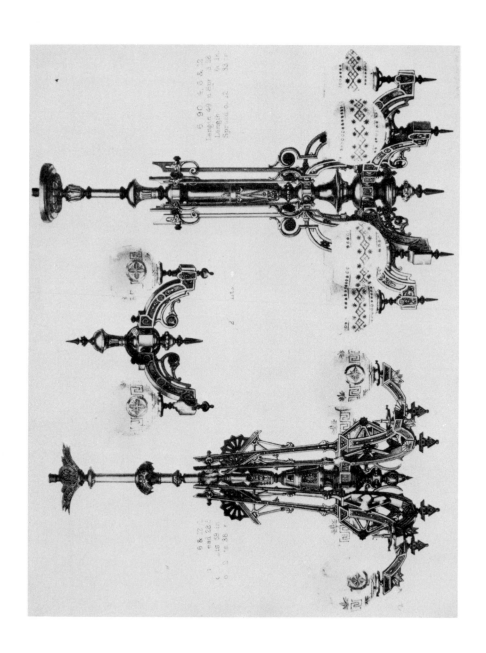

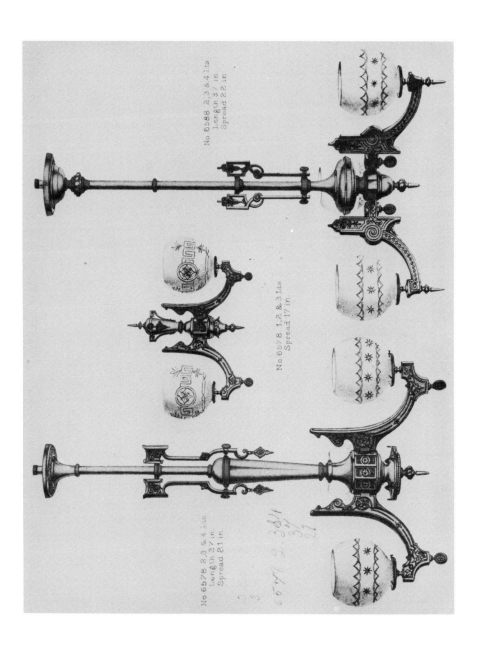

No 6588 2, 3 & 4 Lts
Length 37 in
Spread 22 in

No 6578 1, 2, & 3 Lts
Spread 17 in

No 6578 2, 3 & 4 Lts
Length 37 in
Spread 21 in

25

No. 6282. 2, 3 & 4 Lts.
Length 32 in.
Spread 17 in.

No. 6266. 3, 4 & 6 Lts.
6 Lts. length 45 in. Spread 26 in.
4 "   " 40 in. "   25 in.
3 "   " 39 in. "   24 in.

No. 6450. 2, 3 & 4 Lts.
Length 29 in.
Spread 16½ in.

26

No. 6410. 12 Lights.
Length 59 Inches. Spread 31½ inches.
No. 6410 Gilt.

No. 6492. 1, 2 and 3 Lights.
Spread 17 inches.

No. 6492. 12 Lights.
Length 59 inches. Spread 31 inches.
No. 6492 Gilt.

27

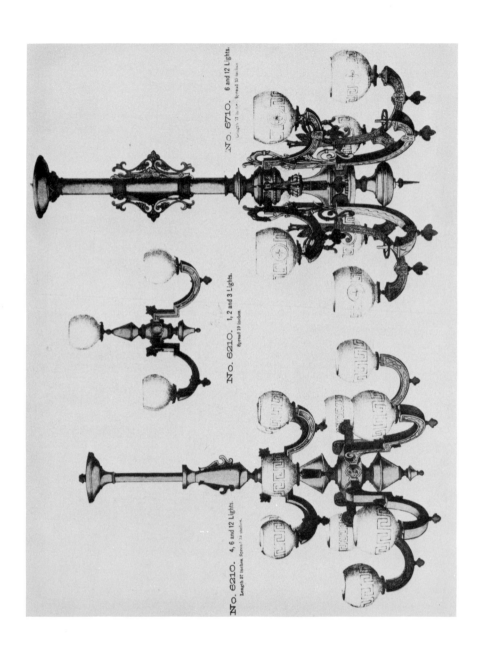

No. 6710. 6 and 12 Lights.
Length 77 inches. Spread 50 inches

No. 6210. 1, 2 and 3 Lights.
Spread 19 inches.

No. 6210. 4, 6 and 12 Lights.
Length 57 inches. Spread 34 inches.

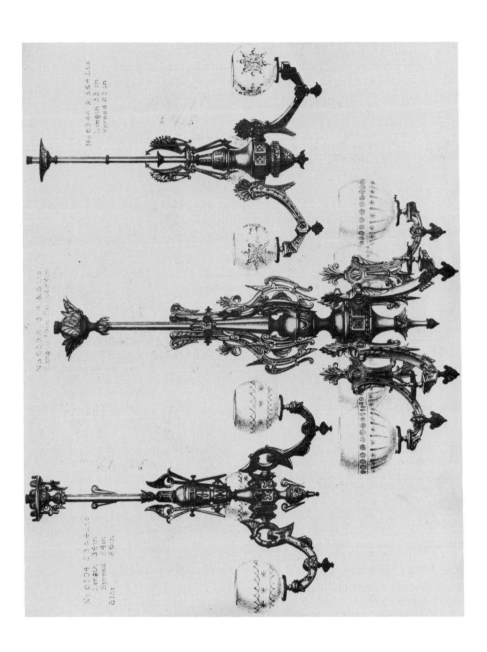

29

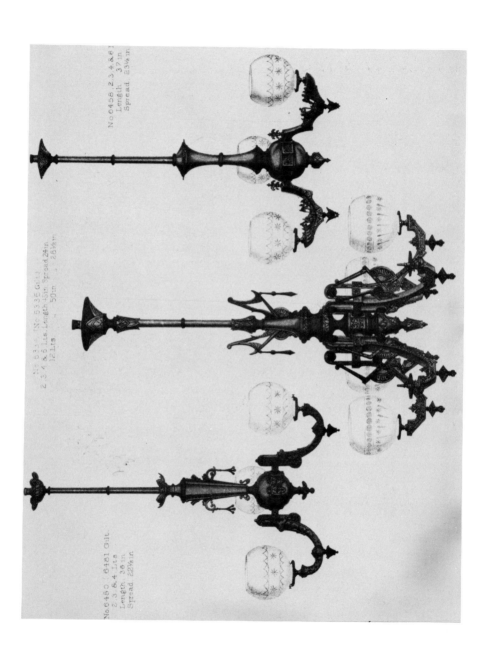

No.6458 2, 3, 4 & 6 Lts
Length 37 in.
Spread 23½ in.

No.5334 No.5335 Gilt
2, 3, 4 & 5 Lts Length 45 in. Spread 24 in.
12 Lts   50 in.   26½ in.

No.6480 6481 Gilt
2, 3 & 4 Lts
Length 36 in.
Spread 22½ in.

30

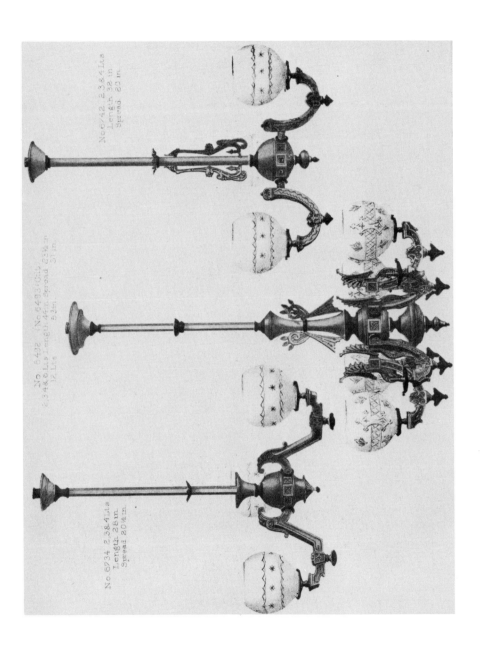

No. 6742. 2, 3 & 4 Lts.
Length 32 in.
Spread 20 in.

No. 6492 No. 6493.600
2, 3 & 6 Lts. Length 44 in. Spread 23½ in.
53 in. 31 in.
12 Lts

No. 6734 2, 3 & 4 Lts.
Length 28 in.
Spread 20½ in.

33

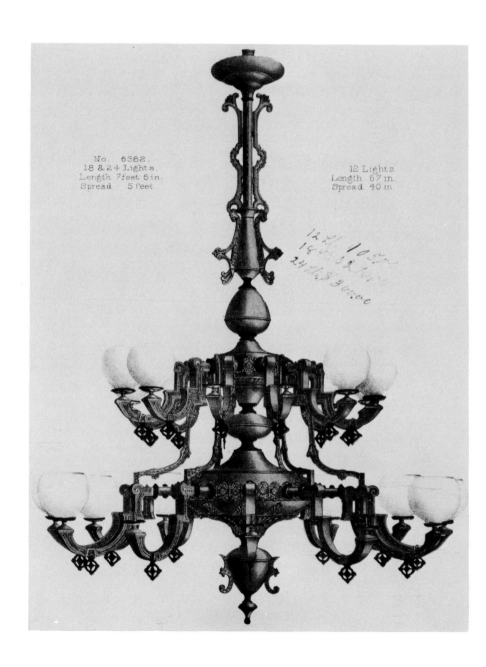

No. 6382.
18 & 24 Lights.
Length 7 feet 6 in.
Spread 5 feet

12 Lights.
Length 67 in.
Spread 40 in

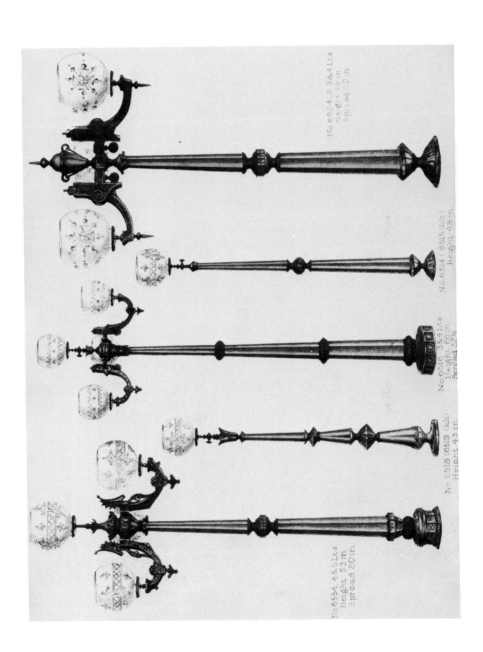

No. 6624. 2, 3 & 4 Lts.
Height 45 in.
Spread 20 in.

No. 6514, 6515 Gilt
Height 45 in.

No. 6516. 3 & 4 Lts.
Height 60 in.
Spread 22½

No. 6518, 6519 Gilt
Height 43 in.

No. 6554. 4 & 5 Lts.
Height 53 in.
Spread 20 in.

No 6292
Height 12½ in.

No 6156
Height 13 in.

No 6536
Height 13½ in.

No 6338
Height 14½ in.

No 6388
Height 15 in.

No 6384 (6385 Gilt)
Height 14½ in.

No 6386 (6387 Gilt)
Height 15 in.

No 5980 (5981 Gilt)
Height 15½ in.

No 6718
Height 12¾ in.

No 6716
Height 13¾ in.

No 6460
Height 15 in.

No 6760
Height 11½ in.

No 6714
Height 14 in.

No 6712
Height 14½ in.

No 6758
Height 12½ in.

No.4936 | 16 in high   No.4934 | 16 in high   No.3346 | 18 in high   No.5684 | 21 in high

ÉTÉ   HIVER

No.4330 | 14 in high   No.8288 | 14 in high   No.5875 | 17 in high   No.6686 | 19 in high

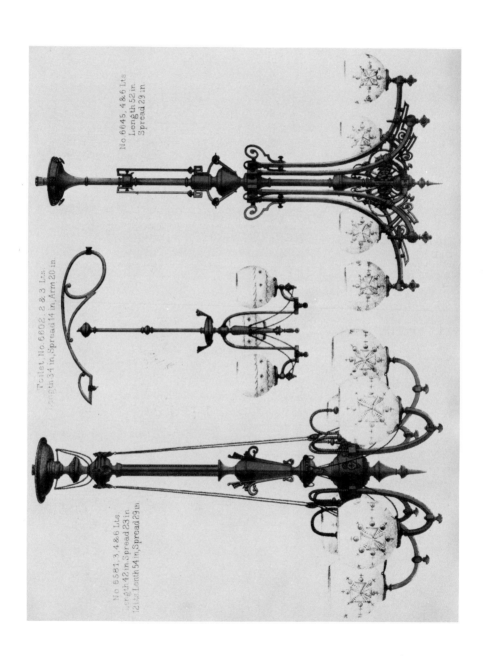

No. 6645. 4 & 6 Lts
Length 52 in.
Spread 29 in.

Toilet, No. 6602. 2 & 3 Lts.
Length 54 in. Spread 14 in. Arm 20 in.

No. 6581. 3, 4 & 6 Lts.
Length 42 in. Spread 23 in.
12 Lt. Lenth 54 in. Spread 29 in.

38

No. 6628. 4 & 6 Lts.
Length 53½ in.
Spread 36 in.

No. 6654. 1, 2 & 3 Lts.
Spread 21 in.

No. 6522. 3, 4 & 6 Lts.
Length 48 in.
Spread 28 in.

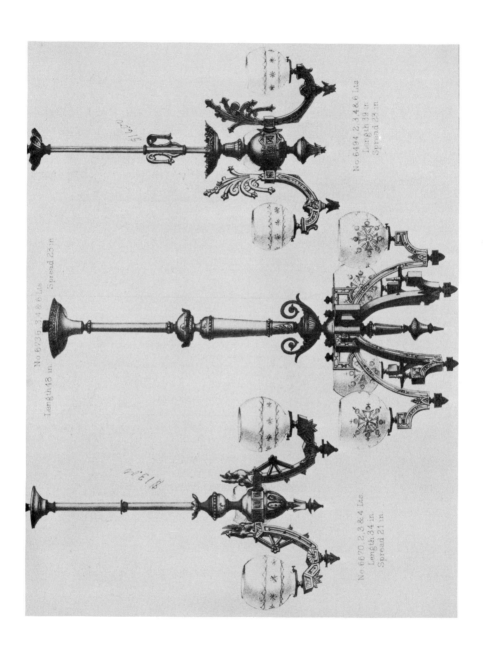

No. 6494. 2, 3, 4 & 6 Lts
Length 39 in.
Spread 23 in.

No. 6736. 2, 4 & 6 Lts.
Length 48 in.   Spread 23 in.

No. 6670. 2, 3 & 4 Lts.
Length 34 in.
Spread 21 in.

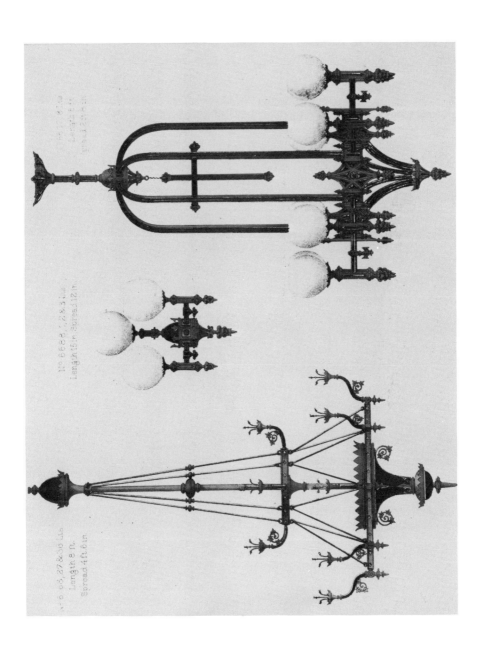

41

Nº 6528, 6 & 9 Lts.
Length 26 in.
Spread 19 in.

Nº 6770, 6 & 9 Lts.
Length 22 in.
Spread 19 in.

42

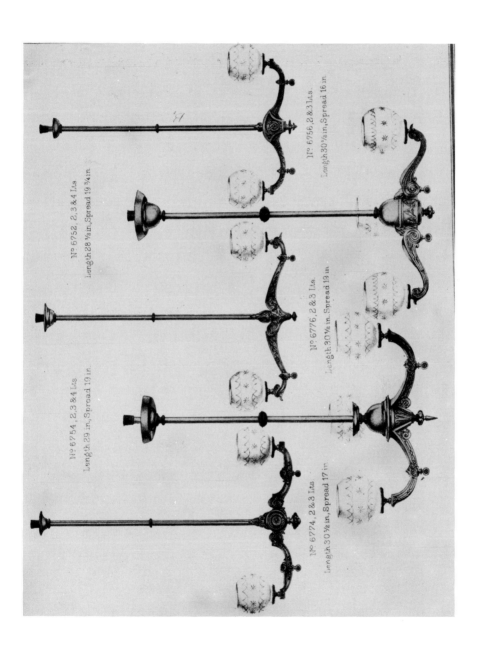

Nº 6752, 2, 3 & 4 Lts.
Length 28½ in., Spread 19¾ in.

Nº 6756, 2 & 3 Lts.
Length 30½ in., Spread 16 in.

Nº 6754, 2, 3 & 4 Lts.
Length 29 in., Spread 19 in.

Nº 6776, 2 & 3 Lts.
Length 30½ in., Spread 19 in.

Nº 6774, 2 & 3 Lts.
Length 30½ in., Spread 17 in.

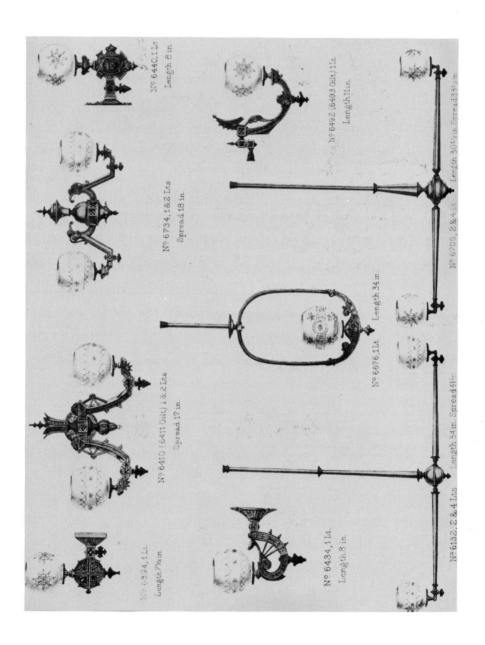

Nº 6440, 1 Lt.
Length 8 in.

Nº 6492 (6493 Gilt) 1 Lt.
Length 11 in.

Nº 6734, 1 & 2 Lts
Spread 18 in.

Nº 6410 (6411 Gilt) 1 & 2 Lts.
Spread 17 in.

Nº 6676, 1 Lt.   Length 34 in.

Nº 6334, 1 Lt.
Length 7½ in.

Nº 6434, 1 Lt.
Length 8 in.

Nº 6700, 2 & 4 Lts.   Length 30½ in. Spread 33½ in.

Nº 6132, 2 & 4 Lts.   Length 34 in. Spread 41 in.

44

Hitchcock Lamp Co., 1887

Robert Hitchcock was born in 1832 in Wolfe Island, Ontario. In 1848 he emigrated to Watertown, N.Y., where he was apprenticed to a jeweler and watchmaker. At the end of his apprenticeship he became a partner in the local establishment. In 1863 he left Watertown, moving first to Boston, Mass., and then to Bristol, Conn., where, as a partner in Jones & Hitchcock, he engaged in the manufacture of lamps and clock works. In 1868 he first patented a kerosene lamp utilizing a forced draft to increase combustion.

In 1872 he returned to Watertown to organize the Hitchcock Lamp Co. Evidently development and perfection of the lamp design required several years, for production did not begin before 1876. The Hitchcock lamp featured a forced draft created by a small fan driven by a clock spring. The lamp was wound like a clock, once a day, with a key. Because of the steady draft produced by the fan, the lamp was virtually smokeless and no chimney was needed. Despite these obvious advantages, its relatively high cost kept the Hitchcock lamp from universal popularity. It was, however, extensively used in public places.

The Hitchcock Lamp Co. must have enjoyed a substantial foreign trade among those willing to pay for high quality. Its 1887 catalog was printed in four languages, although only the pages in English have been reproduced here. All the plates from the catalog have been reproduced with the exception of five. One duplicates the chandelier shown on pages 64 and 65 in a four-light version; two repeat the chandelier on page 66, showing that it was also available with three or four lights; the fourth duplicates page 67 in a four-light version; the other is the three-light equivalent of the chandelier shown on pages 69 and 70 All the lamps shown exhibit the same basic form for the base enclosing the clockwork mechanism, the font and the burner. This basic form was then mounted in various ways to serve as table lamp, bracket, student lamp, hanging lamp or chandelier.

Toward the end of the century, in the face of competition from gas and electric light, the company was reorganized as the Jefferson Brass Co., and other products were added to its line. It probably continued to produce lamps until 1899. In that year Robert Hitchcock retired from the company, granting a license to manufacture his lamp to the New Haven Clock Co., of New Haven, Conn., and the F. H. Lovell Co., of New York City. These companies continued to make Hitchcock lamps until 1905.

THE

HITCHCOCK LAMP

HITCHCOCK LAMP CO., Sole Manufacturers.

MANUFACTORY AND OFFICE:

WATERTOWN, New York, U. S. A.

—Incorporated 1873.—

CASH CAPITAL : $150,000.

HON. ROSWELL P. FLOWER, *President*, 52 BROADWAY, NEW YORK.

ROBERT HITCHCOCK, *Vice-President and Secretary*, WATERTOWN, N. Y.

J. W. MOAK, *Treasurer.*

Patents taken out by Robert Hitchcock from 1868 to 1887,

AS FOLLOWS:

Feb. 25, 1868; Jan. 7, 1873; Dec. 2, 1873; April 23, 1872; Aug. 12, 1873; Dec. 22, 1874; Nov. 30, 1880; July 20, 1886; also in England, France, Belgium, Canada and United States. Patents pending now in all countries of the world.

THIS LAMP IS MEETING WITH SUCCESS ALL OVER THE WORLD.

HUNDREDS OF THOUSANDS OF THEM ARE NOW IN USE IN EUROPE, ASIA, MEXICO, NORTH AND SOUTH AMERICA, AND THE COAST OF AFRICA.

WE SOLICIT ORDERS DIRECT WITH OUR FACTORY,

As we have now elaborate styles, a beautiful factory fully equipped, and a heavy foreign trade.

LAMPS AND FIXTURES OF THE FINEST GOLD COLOR THROUGHOUT, OR NICKELED.

RAILROAD, SHIP AND STEAMER LAMPS. TABLE, WALL AND HANGING LAMPS.

NO SHADES OR CHIMNEYS NEEDED WITH ANY OF OUR LAMPS.

January 1st, 1887.

46

OUR LAMPS

WIND UP ON THE BOTTOM, "STEM WINDERS," TO BE GENUINE HAVE THE NAME

HITCHCOCK LAMP

STAMPED UPON THE LAMP.

THE BEST IN THE WORLD
for Burning Kerosene.

No Globe, No Chimney, No Substitute for either, No Smoke, No Odor, No Danger. Explosion Impossible. No Glass required. No Noise. Burns Open like Gas. Does not heat the face, quite superior for reading and Sewing. Has not the appearance of a Conflagration nor a Moonlight. Not the result of accidental discovery, but long patient effort and an understanding of the laws of combustion.

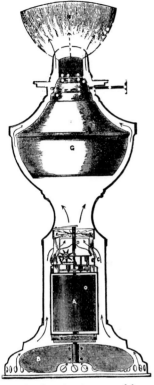

TO those who are not familiar with its principle, a very brief description and diagram will be sufficient to give an understanding.

Combustion is created by a fan driven by clock-work secreted in the base of the lamp, and wound up by means of a key which is attached to the works, and when once wound up drives the fan noiselessly and forces the air into the flame, giving a beautiful white silvery light for about ten hours on being once wound up, thereby dispensing with the chimney. Shades or globes may or may not be used, as desired ; same as gas.

A is clock-work which goes ten hours when fully wound up by the key *B*. This drives by a series of wheels the fan *E E*, which delivers a constant current of air in the directions marked by the arrows. This air circulates around the oil receiver *G*, keeping it cool, and in its upward course impinges upon the flame *H*, as it passes through the burner. The flame is thereby sufficiently oxygenated to give the fullest volume of light—the force of the mechanism being adjusted for that purpose, and giving to tinted fabrics the proper appearance by night.

There are unscrupulous men who secretly use the engravings of our lamp, but without our name upon the lamp. You cannot be mistaken if you find the name

"HITCHCOCK LAMP" stamped on the cone or burner. Not any are genuine Hitchcock lamps without this name.

All circulars without the medals of Franklin Institute and Centennial are not ours.

These medals mean a great deal and cannot be "obtained" from this board of scientists without true merit and much waiting, and often not then if not of importance to the welfare of all.

This lamp gives much more light than a chimney lamp using the same size wick, consumes less oil and has none of the indistinctness of other lamps, the flame standing out upon the lamp like gas; economical in burning, as no smoke means more light, and no chimney means also more light for the same money, saving also in the price of chimneys, and none to clean; gives a light equal to a six-foot gas burner, at one-tenth the cost; makes no shadow upon the ceiling or wall; no tremulous shadow as in gas—it withstands a sudden blast of wind; will burn in a very cold or warm apartment equally well; is compact, cleanly and portable—gives 15-candle power and much more if desired; cannot explode, being all metal and strong. (See diagram.) Upsetting will neither break nor spill it, the oil tank being surrounded by a blast of air is kept cool; is protected from dust, charred wick, snuff ball and burned matches; gives great uniformity and steadiness of the volume of light throughout many hours burning; is very durable, being so strongly made that it is not liable to get out of order; has withstood the wear and tear, shaking, dust, grit and violent use on railroads and government ships without injury or disuse for years. This lamp is also fitted up for burning heavy oils, and is adopted by sleeping-car companies, and the United States Government has many in its service; the ships of polar expeditions were fitted out with them.

The old four-hour lamp was made in New York City twenty years ago by Mr. Hitchcock, and patented in 1868, and 20,000 Mechanical Lamps then and shortly after introduced. Since that time to the present, many changes and improvements were made and patents taken out by him without relinquishing the business, but one steady increase of uninterrupted successful inventions for twenty years. This long, arduous experience should give confidence in the honesty of the workmanship. Patents are now pending in every country on earth where there are such laws. The business has grown from a few hundred per year to many thousands per year. The present lamp being the outgrowth of the past, we caution all manufacturers, dealers and users against infringement of our patents; we have prosecuted several thus far, and will not hesitate in the future; all such are liable to suit.

When broken lamps are to be repaired, send works to us by mail at a trifling cost, or send for card showing parts and prices of the part desired. Every thing is interchangeable.

HITCHCOCK LAMP CO.

HITCHCOCK LAMP COMPANY, Sole Manufacturers and Proprietors,

WATERTOWN, New York, U. S. A.

48

DIRECTIONS

FOR USING THE

Hitchcock House and Store Lamp.

PLEASE READ THESE DIRECTIONS CAREFULLY.

Wind the lamp at the bottom and to a FULL STOP every time that it is wanted for use, if but for ONE-HALF HOUR; wind it until it will wind no more; it will not WEAR OUT, for the longer it runs the better it is. Wind the key at any time if extra light be required.

In filling the lamp, pull off the cone, unscrew the wick tube by LEVER that is used for turning up the wick, as the lever is made unusually strong for that purpose.

Always take the tank part off when TRIMMING and FILLING. Turn the stand upside down and tap it with the hand, so that any dirt or dust that may be lodged in it will be shaken out, leaving the stand upside down to drain while filling and trimming the top part.

Be sure that your burner and oil tank are pressed down TIGHT; if they are not, your light will not work satisfactorily.

Do not pour hot or cold water into the works to clean them.

It will smoke only under three circumstances: *When it is not wound up. When the wick is too short and does not touch the oil. When the flame is turned too high.*

This lamp will give a BETTER LIGHT than GAS or any other KEROSENE LAMP made, but there is a "limit to the size of the flame." It should not be turned up so HIGH that it flickers, but to the point where it gives the beautiful, clear, white, steady light.

Do NOT BLOW the light out, but TURN DOWN the wick until it goes out, and leave it down until you want to use it again, thereby saving all odor.

In lighting the lamp, do not touch the wick with the match, as it spoils the beauty of the light.

Should any clippings (after long use) lodge between the tank and top, remove them with a feather. Where two or more lamps are used, don't exchange tanks or burners.

In trimming the lamps cut off only a part of the charred wick, clean the gum off the wick tube with fresh oil, throw away the old wick and put in a new one; the wick acts as a strainer for all the oil and becomes foul.

If any lamp is filled quite too full with cold oil, when the oil becomes warm it will overflow and give suspicion that the lamp leaks.

Better to fill the lamp every day, gives a finer light; a new wick will not burn so well in any lamp unless it has been once trimmed.

The wicks for the HITCHCOCK LAMP are made full standard size and of the best material, which we send by post everywhere; the ordinary wick will burn very well, but not so fine. Should our lamps meet with accident, the works can be sent to us by post at a small cost, otherwise order the parts as herein illustrated.

TO TAKE APART FOR REPAIRS ONLY.

Take off the top of the lamp, turn up the bottom, take out the screw in the key, or unscrew the key, unscrew two more screws, turn up the lamp and pull out the movement.

To TAKE THE MOVEMENT APART. — First put on the key, hold the movement in one hand and the key in the other. Put back the clicks and let the movement turn slowly around in the hand until there is no power left. It will then be safe to take apart.

By fully following these simple directions, your lamp will last *twenty-five years*. Keep these directions for further reference, and if your lamp should ever accidentally get out of order, you will have then to refer to

HITCHCOCK LAMP CO., Watertown, New York, U. S. A.

PRICE-LIST OF HITCHCOCK LAMPS IN FINE GOLD COLORED BRASS, OR NICKEL.

No Shade Rings or Glass included, unless mentioned complete.   This Price-list takes the place of all previous ones whether written, printed, or verbal.

No. 0	Table Lamp or Stand Lamp....................Each..	$ 6 00
No. 1	Store Lamp or Bracket Lamp ....Each..	6 50
No. 2	Harp with Lamp..............................Each..	6 35
No. 3	Harp with Lamp..............................Each..	8 75
No. 4	Lamp with attachment for gas fixture.........Each..	6 30
No. 5	Table Lamp, ornamental, brass finish.........Each..	12 00
No. 6	Table Lamp, decorated, brass finish..........Each..	7 25
No. 7	Bracket and Lamp, with Reflector.............Each..	10 00
No. 8	Student Lamp, single.........................Each..	11 70
No. 9	Student Lamp, double.........................Each..	17 50
No. 10	Vase Lamp (hammered) Nickel, Old Gold and Bronze,	10 50
" 11	Vase Lamp (Grecian) Nickel, Old Gold and Bronze.	10 50
" 12	Vase Lamp (Grecian) Nickel, Old Gold and Bronze.	10 50
" 13	Vase Lamp (hammered) Nickel, Old Gold and Bronze,	10 50
No. 14	Faience Lamp (Ivy Oak)......................	12 00
" 15	Faience Lamp (Roman)........................	13 50
" 16	Faience Lamp (Extra Roman)..................	17 00
" 17	Faience Lamp, figured bronze base...........	
" 18	Faience Lamp, figured bronze base	
" 19	Faience Lamp, figured bronze base	
No. 20	Extension Library Lamp, with prisms....complete..	20 00
" 21	Extension Library Lamp.............complete	11 50
" 22	Double Extension Library Lamp......complete	12 25
" 23	Hanger and Lamp (no extension)....complete	10 00
No. 24	Extension Chandelier with lamps....2 lights..	27 00
" 25	Extension Chandelier with lamps....3 lights..	37 50
" 26	Extension Chandelier with lamps....4 lights..	46 50
No. 27	Extension Chandelier with lamps....2 lights..	35 00
" 28	Extension Chandelier with lamps....3 lights..	48 00
" 29	Extension Chandelier with lamps....4 lights..	60 00
No. 30	Extension Chandelier with lamps....3 lights..	45 50
" 31	Extension Chandelier with lamps....4 lights..	55 50
No. 34	Extension Chandelier and lamps, drop....3 lights..	60 00
No. 38	Extension Chandelier with lamps....2 lights..	32 00
" 39	Extension Chandelier with lamps....3 lights..	43 00
" 40	Extension Chandelier with lamps....4 lights..	53 00
No. 41	Bracket and Lamp......................1 light.....	$12 00
" 42	Bracket and lamps.....................2 lights..	25 00
" 43	Bracket and lamps.....................3 lights..	33 00
" 44	Bracket, double joint.................1 light..	14 50
" 45	Extension Library Lamp, Prisms.......complete..	18 50
" 46	Extension Library Lamp...............complete..	17 00
No. 105	Lard Oil, Box Lamp, Bulk Head (U. S. N.), Each..	36 00
No. 112	Lard Oil, Car Bracket Lamp..............Each..	30 00
No. 113	Lard Oil, Cabin Lamp complete...........Each..	36 00
No. 114	Lard Oil, Center Car Lamp complete......Each..	36 00
No. 115	5-inch Globe Rings......................Doz.	2 50
No. 116	7-inch Shade Rings......................Doz.	2 88
No. 117	10-inch Shade Holders...................Doz.	4 60
No. 118	(B) Kerosene Lamp Wicks, per gross.	1 00
No. 119	(No. 1) Lard Oil Wicks, per gross.	2 50
No. 120	5x7½ inch Opal Globes...................Doz.	4 25
No. 122	5x7½ inch Opal Globes, decorated........Doz.	12 00
No. 123	5x7½ inch Round, Etched Globes..........Doz.	8 00
No. 124	Crown Etched Globes.....................Doz.	17 25
No. 125	Cut and Polished Globes (cone)..........Doz.	80 00
No. 126	Cut and Polished Globes (round).........Doz.	110 00
No. 127	Crown Globe, Iridescent and Gilt........Doz.	60 00
No. 128	7-inch Shade, Opal (wide top)...........Doz.	1 60
No. 129	10-inch Shade, Opal, French.............Doz.	4 60
No. 200	14-inch Shades (dome) tinted and decorated....Doz.	18 50
No. 201	14-inch Shades (dome) decorated.........Doz.	14 50
No. 202	14-inch Shades (cone) tinted and decorated....Doz.	16 00
No. 203	14-inch Shades (cone) decorated.........Doz.	12 00
No. 204	3 or 3½ inch Smoke Bells................Doz.	1 75
No. 205	5-inch Smoke Shades.....................Doz.	3 25
No. 206	Prisms............................per hundred..	7 50
No. 207	Clock Works for Hitchcock Lamp.	

Trimmings not included unless mentioned complete.
Glass subject to slight change in price, not included unless mentioned complete.

Watertown, New York, U. S. A., June 1st, 1887.

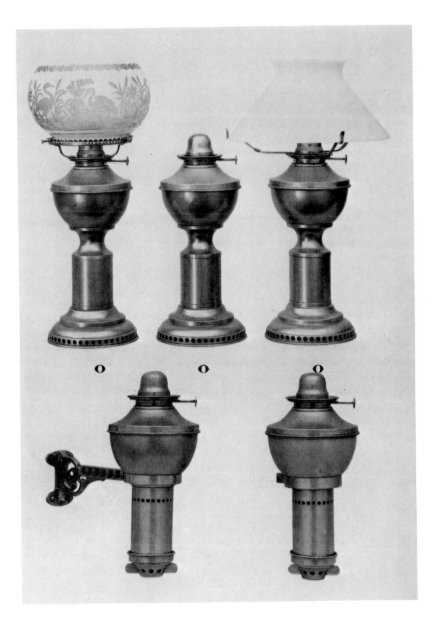

O   O   O

1   4

51

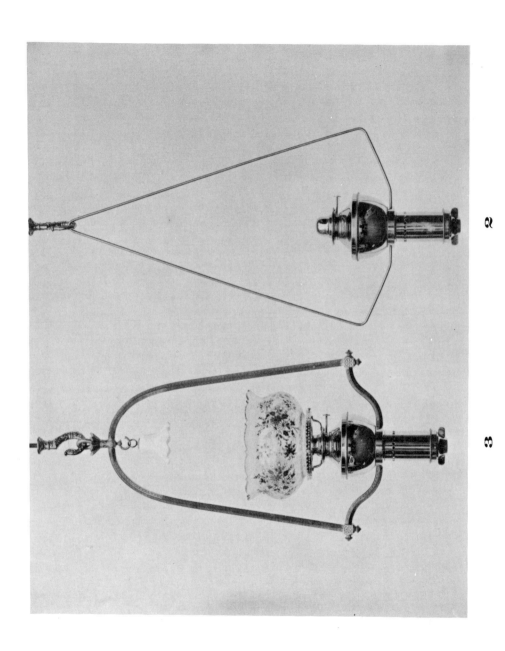

5

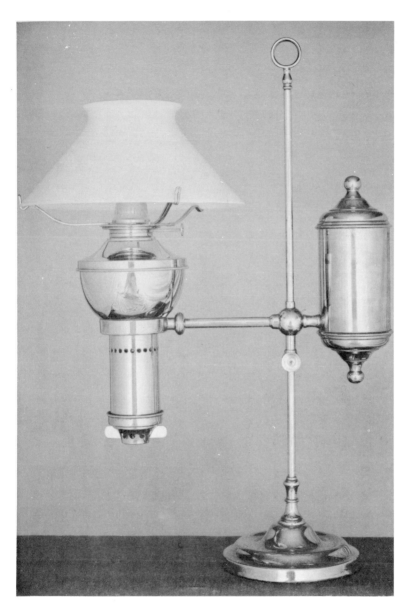

8

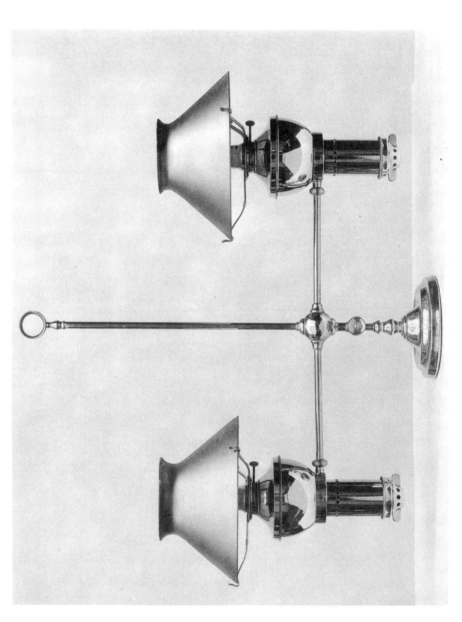

10   11   12   13

14 16 15

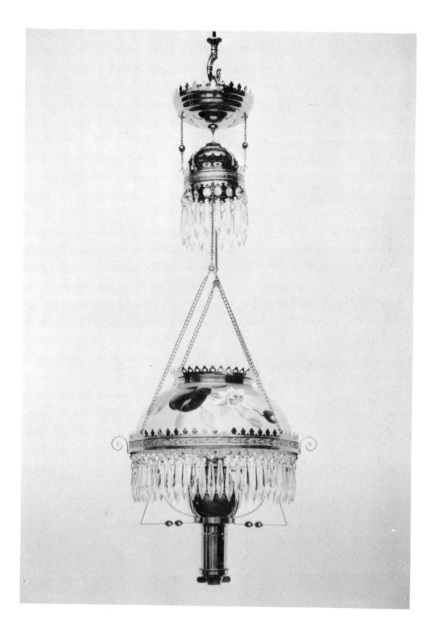

20

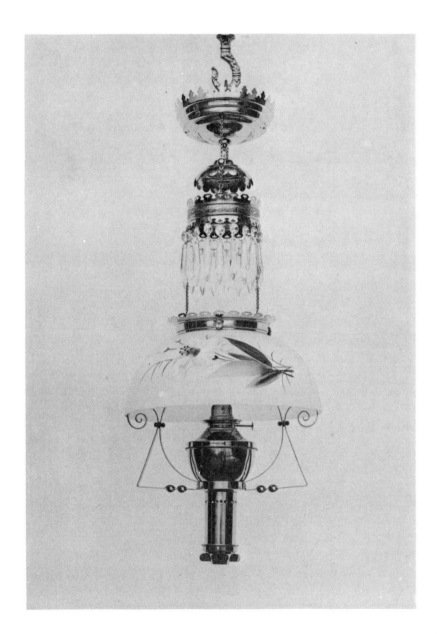

45

46

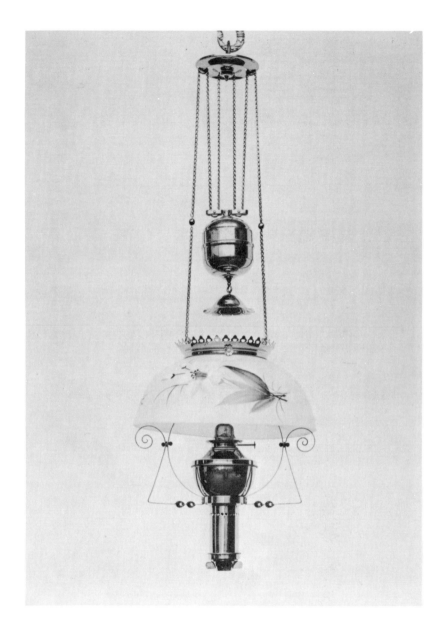

22

23

24

25

27

30

34

38

40

41 42 43 44

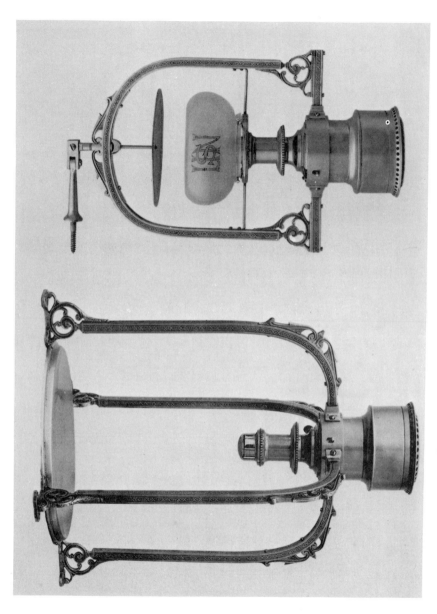

113

114

105

112

73

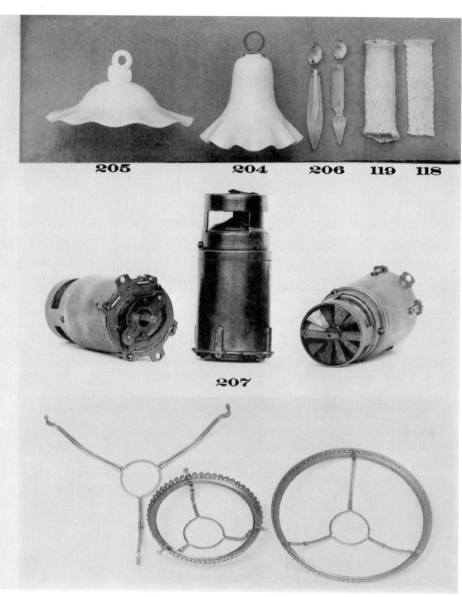

205   204   206 119 118

207

117 115   116

King Glass Co., c. 1890

The King Glass Company, whose special supplementary catalog for lamps is reproduced here, had roots in the Pittsburgh glass-producing area going back to pre-Civil War days. The parent firm, founded in 1859, was the Cascade Glass Co. In 1864, this was succeeded by Johnson, King & Co. Subsequent name changes, reflecting changes in ownership and management, were King, Son & Co. in 1869 and King Glass Co. in 1884. In 1891, King was one of the 18 Ohio and Pennsylvania companies merged to form the United States Glass Company.

This catalog, originally bound with others from the United States Glass Co., was probably the first one issued after the merger. Since the name on the title page is that of King Glass, rather than the "Factory K" designation used by the United States Glass Co., the catalog was probably prepared before the merger took place.

King Glass was basically a manufacturer of tableware of all kinds, but, as the catalog makes clear, its selection of lamps was fairly extensive. All the patterns available from King in 1890-91 are included in the following pages. However, five plates, showing the same patterns in different versions, have been omitted. #480 came also as a hand lamp without a foot and as a standing lamp 11, 10¼ and 9¼ inches high. #440 was also available as a footed hand lamp and, standing, in 8, 8½ and 9-inch heights. Numbers 400, 351 and 490 all also came in non-footed hand versions. Numbers 400 and 490 were available as standing lamps 9, 9¾ and 10½ inches high; 351 could be ordered in 8¾, 9½ and 10¼-inch heights.

In the original catalog, #490 was illustrated in color. As a banquet lamp it was available in pale blue, with white opalescent dots, and was shown with a pink shade. In other forms it came in crystal as well as the blue, both with white dots.

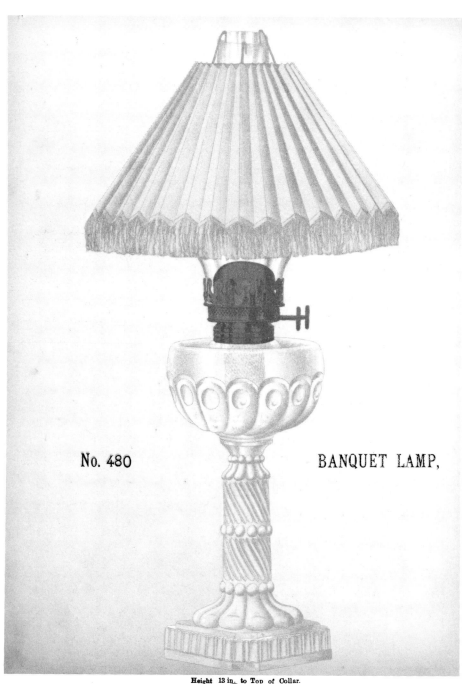

No. 480　　　　　　　　　　　　　　　　　　　BANQUET LAMP,

Height 13 in. to Top of Collar.

76

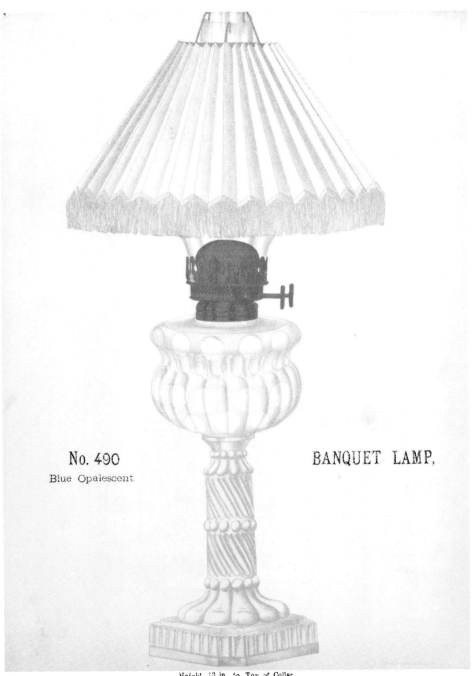

No. 490

Blue Opalescent

BANQUET LAMP,

Height 13 in. to Top of Collar

No. 480 LAMPS.

No. 0—480 Stand.   Height, 7¾ in.

No. 1—480 Footed Hand.

No. 1—480 Stand.   Height, 8⅛ in.

SCALE ½.

No. 0—480 Footed Hand.

No. 2—480 Stand, with A or B Collar.
Height, 8¾ in.

78

No. 440. LAMPS.

No. 0—440 Footed Hand.
5 ¾ in. High.

No. 2—440. Stand, No. 1 or 2 Collar.
9 in. High.

No. 1—440. Stand,
8½ in. High.

No. 1—440 Footed Hand,
5¾ in. High.

No. 0—440 Stand,
8 in. High.

THE CENTRAL LITH. CO. PITTS. PA.

79

No. 400 LAMPS.

E

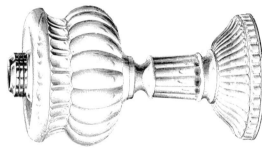

No. 2 — 400. No. 1, or 2. Collar.
8½ in. High.

No. 0 — 400. Foot Hand.
5¼ in. High.

No. 1 — 400.
8 in. High.

No. 1 — 400. Foot Hand.
5¾ in. High.

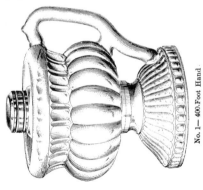

No. 0 — 400.
7½ in. High.

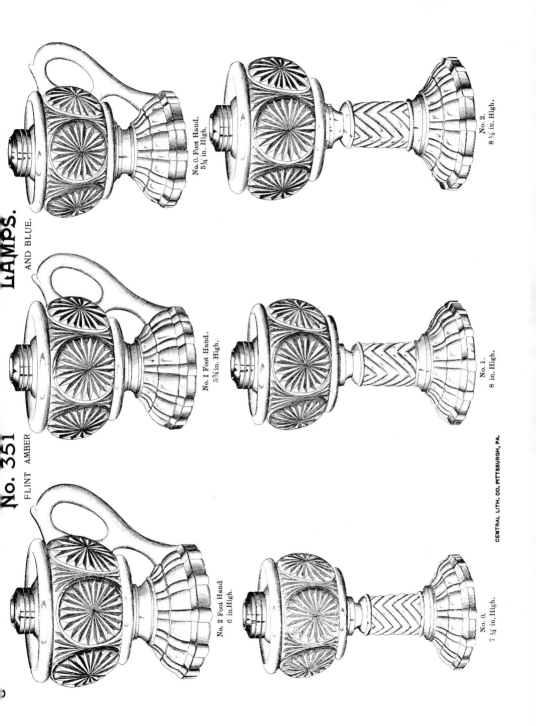

LAMPS.
No. 351
FLINT AMBER AND BLUE.

No. 0. Foot Hand.
5¼ in. High.

No. 2.
8½ in. High.

No. 1 Foot Hand.
5¾ in. High.

No. 1.
8 in. High.

No. 2 Foot Hand.
6 in. High.

No. 0.
7¾ in. High.

CENTRAL LITH. CO. PITTSBURGH, PA.

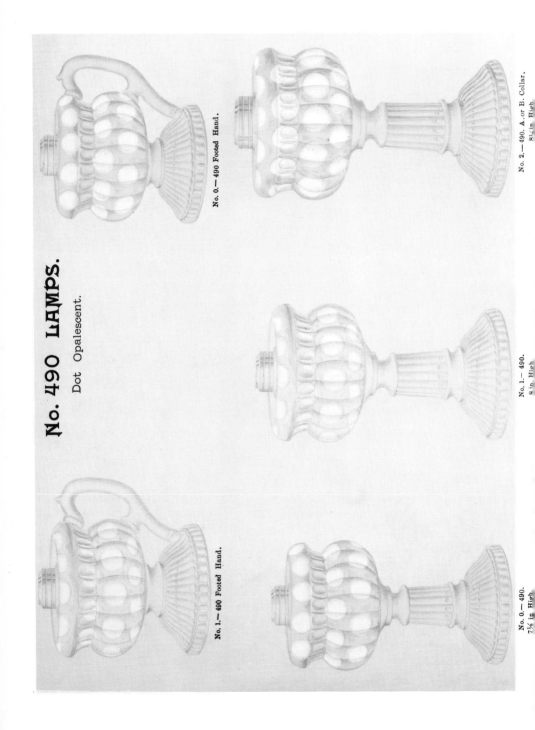

No. 490 Lamps.

Dot Opalescent.

No. 0.—490 Footed Hand.

No. 1.—490 Footed Hand.

No. 2.—490. A. or B. Collar.
8½ in. High.

No. 1.—490.
8 in. High.

No. 0.—490.
7½ in. High.

Bellaire Goblet Co., 1891

As its name indicates, Bellaire, founded in 1878, was chiefly known for its production of drinking glasses, particularly stemmed ware. However, the company also made salvers, compotes, bowls, pitchers and other tableware, bitters bottles, decanters and cruets, as well as novelties. Its selection of lamp bases, as revealed in this catalog, was an extensive one.

In 1891 Bellaire, along with 17 other Pennsylvania and Ohio glass companies, was merged into the United States Glass Co. of Pittsburgh. The company's factories at Findlay and Bellaire, Ohio, were dismantled and production was shifted to Tiffin, Ohio. Under the management of United States Glass, the company was known simply as Factory M.

From the title page of the 1891 catalog supplement, plates from which are reproduced in the following pages, it is obvious that the original catalog was prepared before the merger. The company is referred to as the Bellaire Goblet Co., and the address is given as Findlay, Ohio. The words "U.S. Glass Co. Factory M" have been added with a rubber stamp.

Although the majority of lamps illustrated in the original catalog have been reproduced in the following pages, eight styles have been omitted. All of these bear a marked resemblance to the patterns shown and examples can be identified by their similarity. For instance, #202 is identical with #201, as shown, except that the former offered a font decorated with sharp double ribs and raised diamonds. #234 featured a simulated cut base, like that shown on #311 and #402, but came with a decorated font. #685 was a lamp with a base identical to #684; the only difference was in the font, which featured a basketwork band. #791 had a base like #772, but with a plain font. Again #856 was identical to #858, but with a plain font; it came in crystal only. #857 also featured the same base; its font was ribbed. #877 had a base like #950. The lower part of the font was fluted, the upper either plain or engraved with a leaf pattern; it was available only in crystal. #207 was the plainest lamp shown, with an inverted saucer-shaped base, concave ringed shaft and globular font.

The imperfections on page 95 reproduce those found in the original catalog.

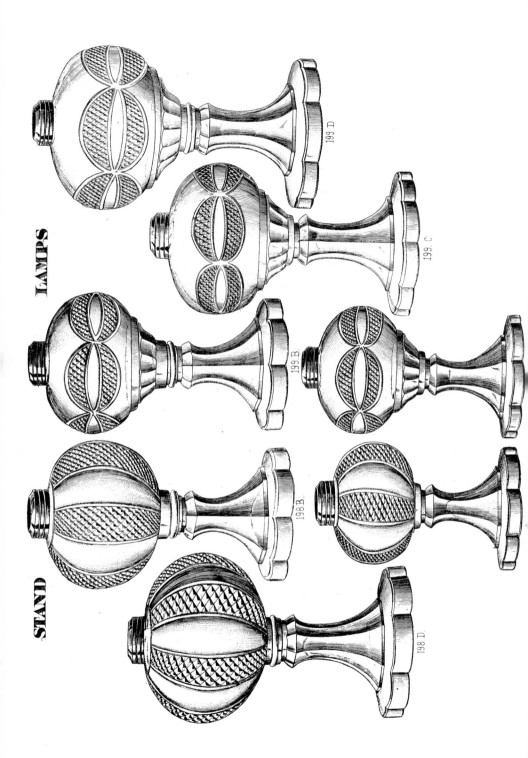

LAMPS

STAND

199 D

199. C.

199. B.

198. B.

198 D.

84

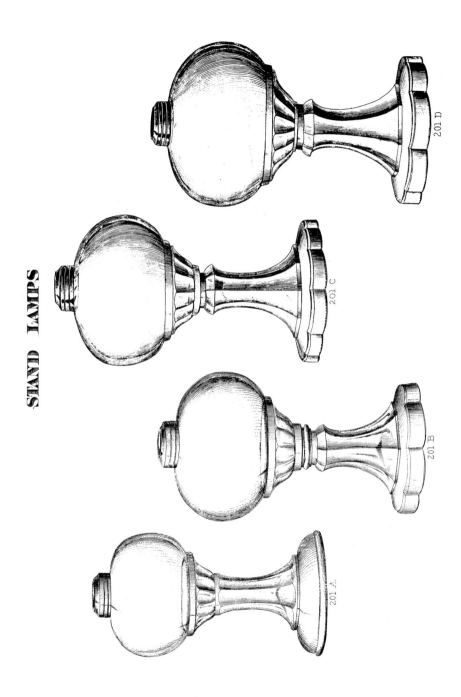

STAND LAMPS

201 D

201 C

201 B

201 A

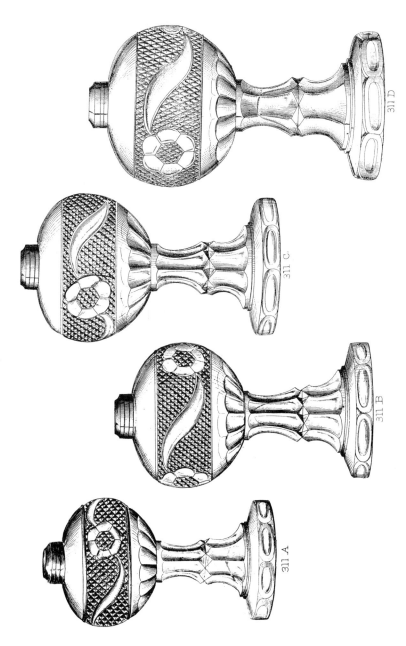

311 A

311 B

311 C.

311 D

STAND LAMPS

402 D

402 C

402 B

486 A

402 A

469 B

87

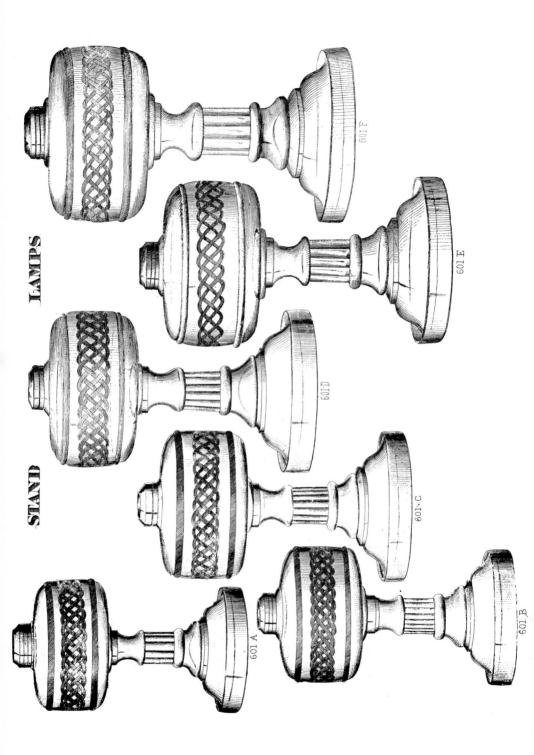

STAND LAMPS

601 A
601 B
601·C
601·D
601 E
601 F

88

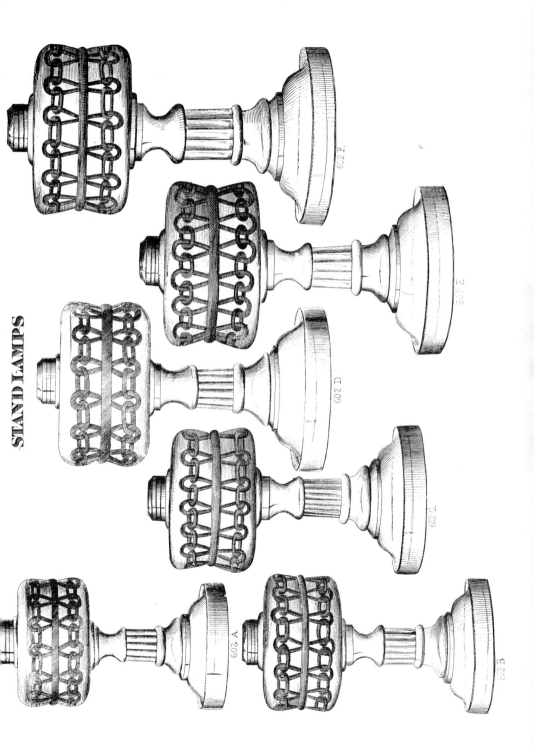

STAND LAMPS

602 F.

602 E.

602 D

602 C.

602 A

602 B

89

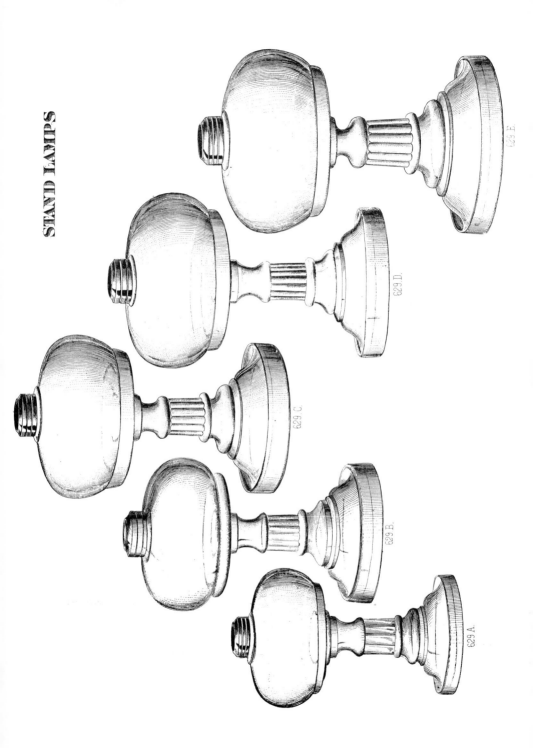

629 E.

629 D.

629 C.

629 B.

629 A.

STAND LAMPS

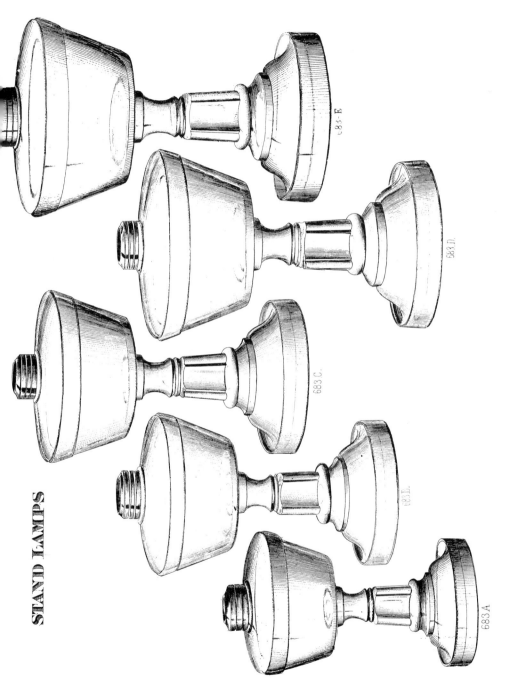

683-E

683.D.

683 C.

683.B.

683 A

91

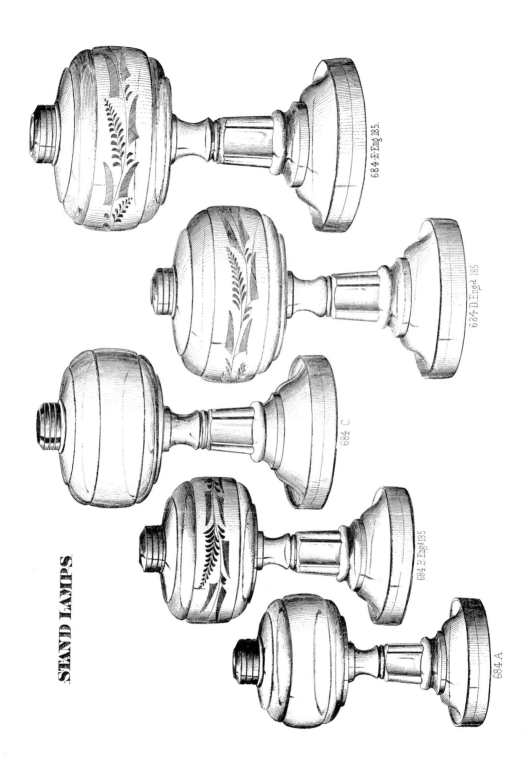

STAND LAMPS

684 F. Eng 185.

684 D. Eng'd 185.

684 C.

684 E. Eng'd 185

684 A

92

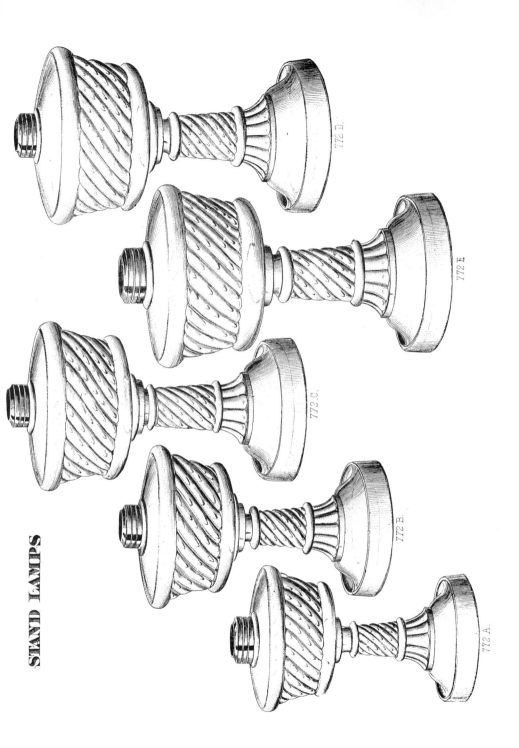

STAND LAMPS

772 D.

772 E.

772 C.

772 B.

772 A.

STAND LAMPS

790 E

790 D

790 C

790 B

790 A

STAND LAMPS.

810 Lamp
Nº 1 or 2 Collar.

810-E-2 Collar

810 E Nº 2 Collar

810-D-1or 2 Collar.

810-C-Eng. 219

810-B-Eng.

810-A.

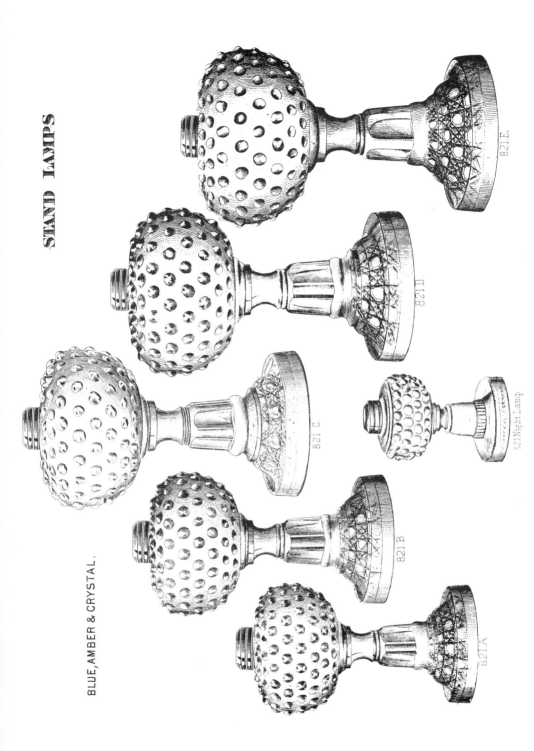

STAND LAMPS

BLUE, AMBER & CRYSTAL.

821 F.

821 D

821 C.

821 Night Lamp

821 B

821 A

96

BLUE, AMBER & CRYSTAL.

Nº 310 Night Lamp. Pressed.

858 E. Nº 2 Collar.

858 D. Nº 1 or 2 Collar.

858 C.

STAND LAMPS

858 B

Nº 300 Night Lamp.

858 A

97

STAND LAMPS

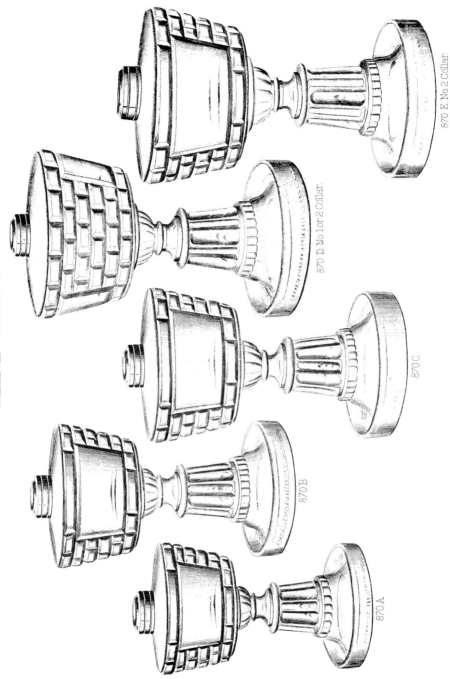

870 E. No 2 Collar.

870 D. No 1 or 2 Collar.

870 C.

870 B

870 A

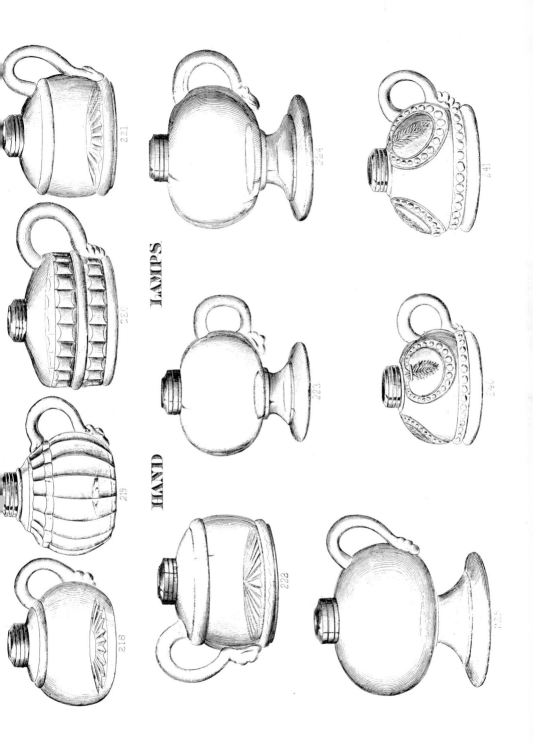

LAMPS

HAND

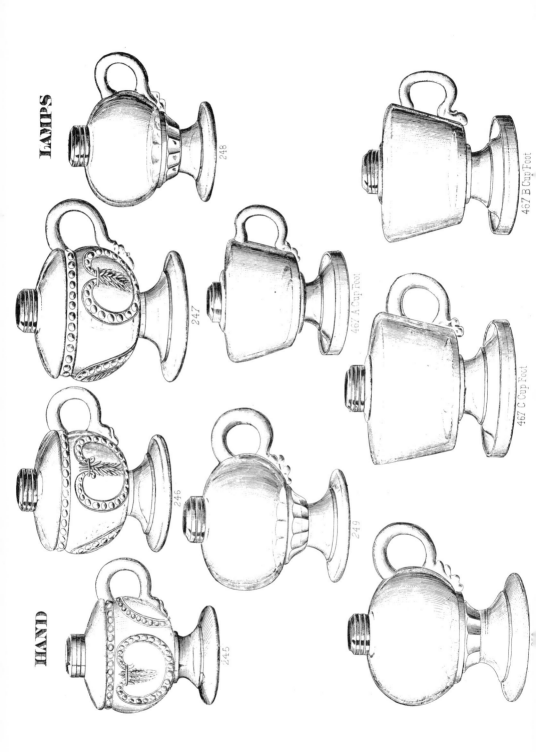

LAMPS

HAND

248

247

246

245

249

467 A Cup Foot

467 B Cup Foot

467 C Cup Foot

100

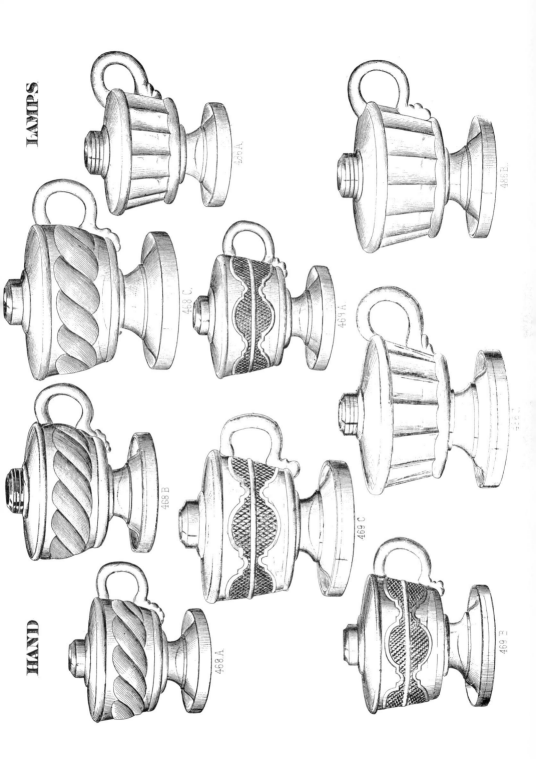

LAMPS

HAND

468 A.

468 B

468 C.

469 A.

469 C

469 B

468 A.

469 B

101

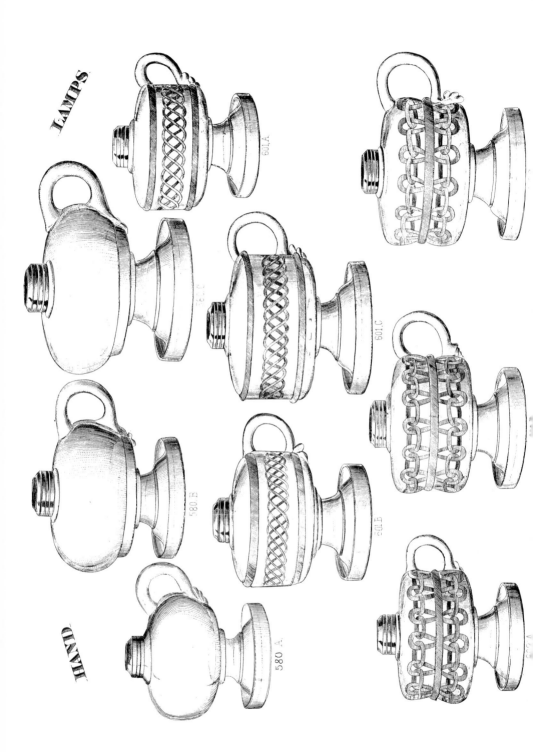

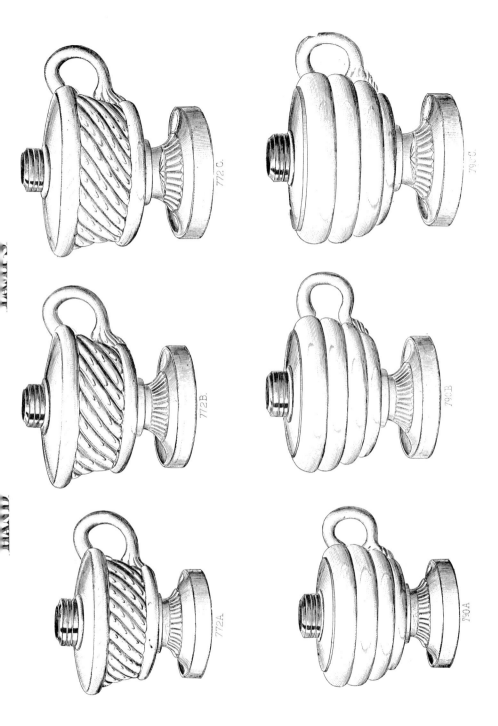

791 C
810 C
791 B
810 B
791 A
810 A

104

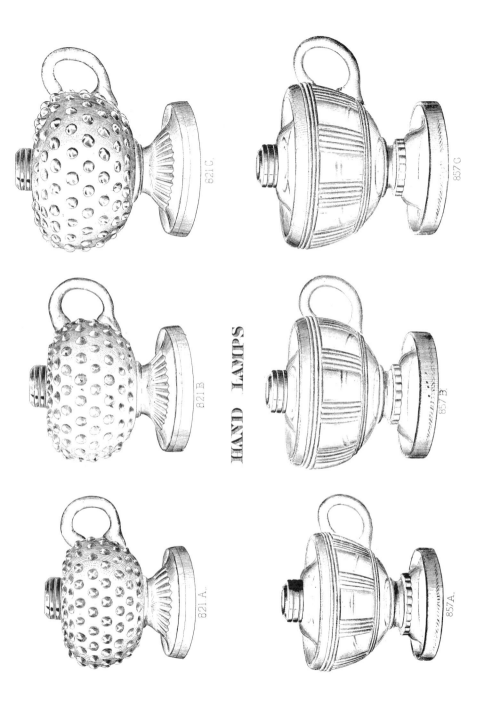

821 C.

857 G.

821 B.

857 B.

HAND LAMPS

821 A.

857 A.

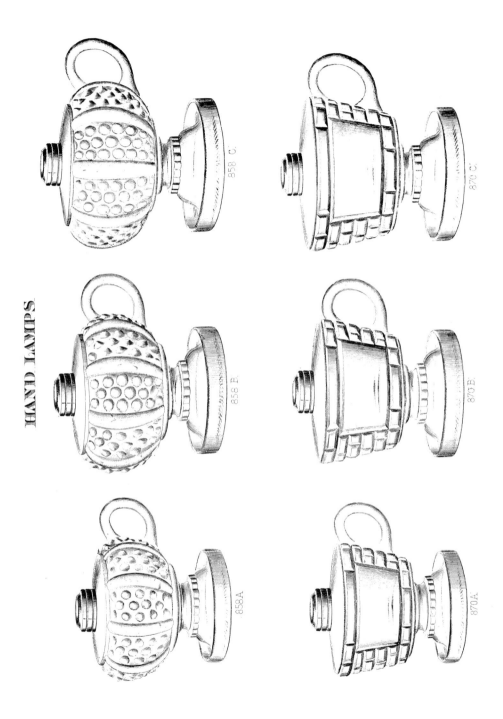

HAND LAMPS

858 C.

870 C.

858 B.

870 B.

858 A.

870 A.

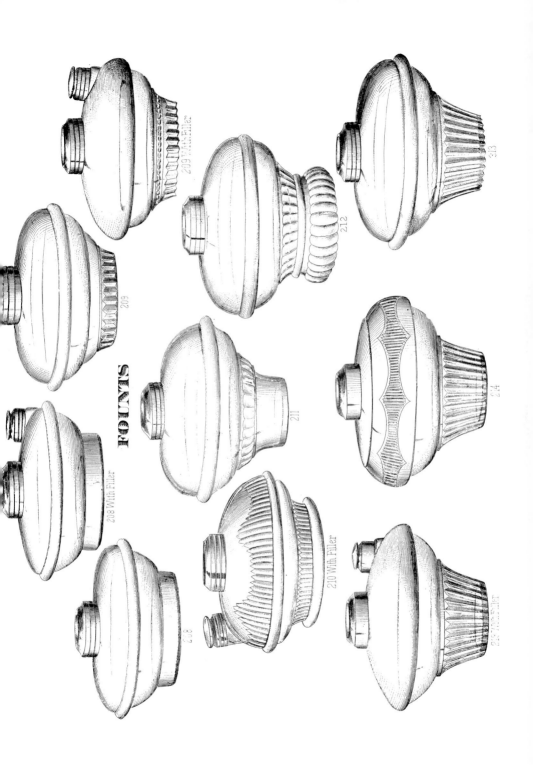

FONTS

208 With Filler
209
209 With Filler
212
213

208
211
214

210 With Filler
210 With Filler

107

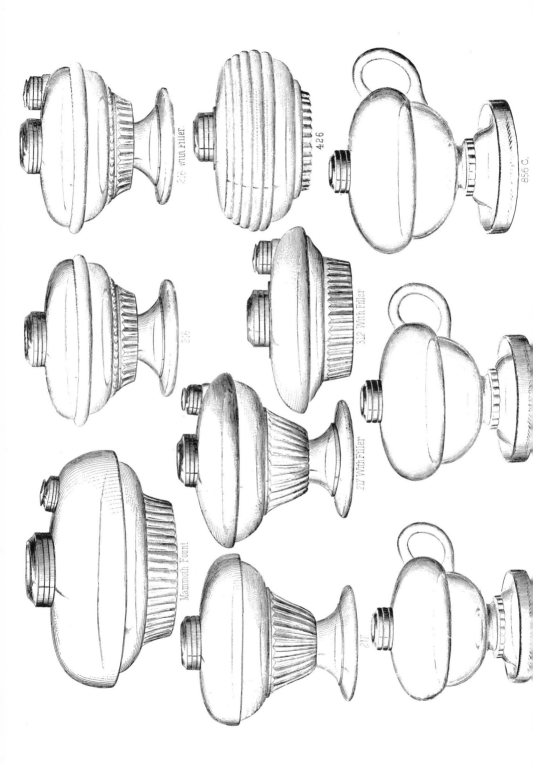

426 with Filler

426

856 C.

426

312 With Filler

Mammoth Fount

217 With Filler

217

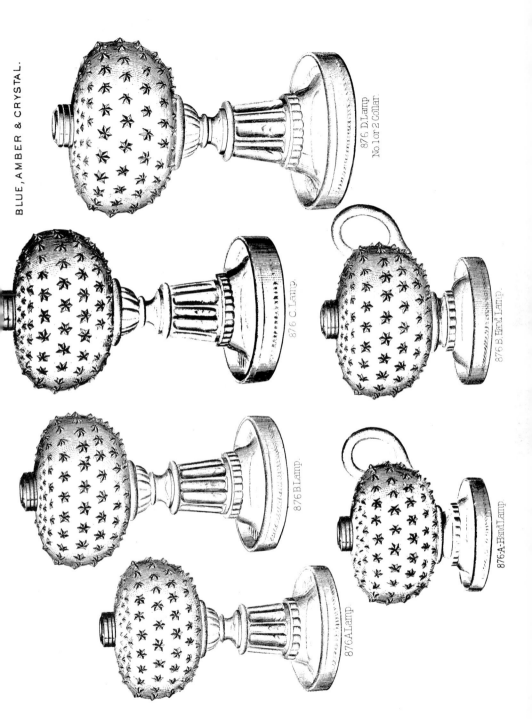

BLUE, AMBER & CRYSTAL.

876 D. Lamp
No 1 or 2 Collar

876 C. Lamp.

876 B. Hand Lamp.

876 B. Lamp.

876 A. Hand Lamp.

876 A. Lamp.

109

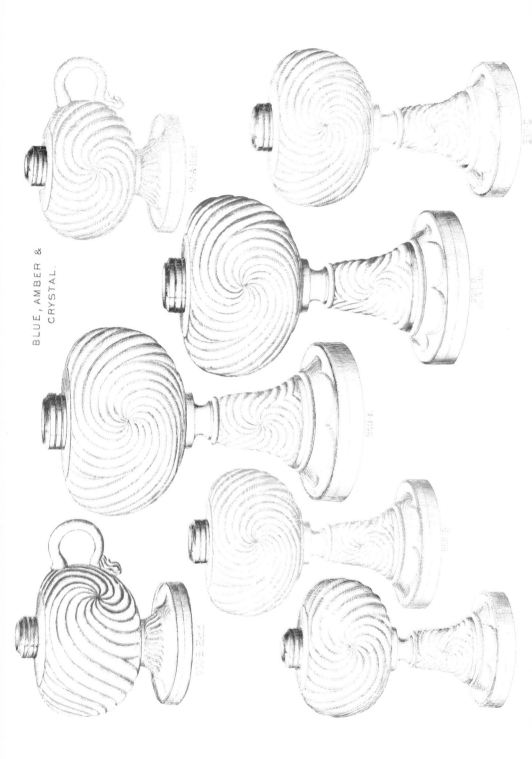

BLUE, AMBER & CRYSTAL.

110

Macbeth-Evans Glass Co., c. 1900

Macbeth-Evans was formed in 1899 by a merger of two major producers of lamp chimneys, one founded in 1869 by Thomas Evans, the other originating in a company formed in 1872 by George A. Macbeth. In the same year the merged company acquired the American Lamp Chimney Co., which owned M. J. Owen's patents on a glass-blowing machine suitable for the production of lamp chimneys. Macbeth-Evans, through mergers and acquisitions, was, at the turn of the century, operating plants in Pittsburgh, and Charleroi, Pa., Marion, Ind., and Todedo, Ohio.

As the country's largest producer of lamp chimneys, Macbeth-Evans made chimneys of plain glass in every shape conceivable for every type of kerosene lamp. When decorative top rims became popular in the 1870's, the parent company of Thomas Evans secured, in 1877, the rights to a patented crimping machine, to produce a "pie crust" edging. The George A. Macbeth Co. patented, in 1883, the "Pearl Top" chimney, in which the top rim was adorned with 36 or 40 glass beads or pearls, the number depending on chimney size.

It was not only decorated rims that were popular in the last quarter of the century. Often chimneys, glass globes or shades, which were also produced by Macbeth-Evans, were etched or painted in colors with designs of wreaths, flowers, landscapes and marine views. These decorated chimneys and shades became popular around 1885. By the late 1880's the Thomas Evans Co. was turning out 4,000,000 decorated pieces a year.

In addition to chimneys, shades and globes, Macbeth-Evans manufactured lighthouse lenses, glass for marine, railroad, and later, automotive, use, and laboratory glassware.

Most of the plates from this slim, undated catalog have been reproduced in the following pages. The pages omitted include three showing lantern globes; one with three examples of railway headlights (these, it was noted, were covered completely in a separate catalog); one displaying a silvered globe reflector; and a final page that offered four opal shades and a globe decorated with iris.

Portable lamps, electric
Railroad signal lamp lenses
Railroad lantern globes, chimneys, etc.
Reflectors, Mangin mirror, for automobile lamps
Reflectors, silvered glass, for bracket
Shades, oil, gas, electric, etc.
Street lamp globes. Tungsten lamp shades, Alba, Monax, etc.

STANDARD BRANDS

The glasses which we manufacture are made in several qualities of glass, each of which is distinguished by a trade-mark etched on each article.

Pearl Glass is a grade peculiar to us, and we hold it superior to all others. The name lead glass is so abused by makers that it no longer means much. The question is: How good is it? That depends on the maker. Our low-grade lead glass we call flint; we even put some lead in our lime glass. We should call that lead if we were disposed to follow the worst examples.

Following are descriptions of the various brands and how they are packed. In connection with each description is illustrated a reproduction of the trade-marks of the different brands. These are listed in order as to quality and package.

TRADE-MARK   TRADE-MARK

MACBETH
No
PEARL GLASS AND
PEARL TOP
PEARL GLASS
MADE IN U.S.A.

Pearl Glass is the metal from which Pearl Glass and Pearl Top glasses are made. There are differences between Pearl Glass and Pearl Top, due to the two forms of top, but not in the glass or in quality; these are alike. Pearl top has a row of pearls around the top, the patent on which has expired. There are other glasses having this ornament now. In the lower grades we refer to similar goods as Crimp Top. There are in the world no other such glasses, in these respects: The glass is tough against heat, it is clear and stays clear, the shape is such as to get full light from the lamps, and the accuracy and fineness of make secure full light.

ZENITH

A high-grade lead glass, packed in square cartons.

KEYSTONE

A high-grade lead glass, same quality as Zenith, but packed in corrugated tubes or hay.

IRON CLAD

A fine flint glass, packed in square cartons.

SUPERIOR

A fine flint glass, same quality as Iron Clad, but packed in corrugated tubes or hay.

CRESCENT

A first quality lime glass, packed in square cartons.

EMPIRE

A first quality lime glass, same as Crescent, but packed in corrugated tubes or hay.

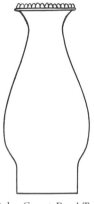

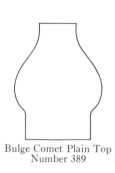

Bulge Comet Plain Top
Number 389

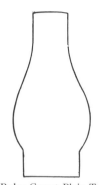

Bulge Comet Pearl Top

Bulge Comet Plain Top

Sun Bulb or Bulge Comet—Pearl Top
For Sun Burners, Eureka, Queen Anne, etc

Number	Code Word	Description	Diameter Inches Fitting	Diameter Inches Bulb	Height Inches	Standard Package	Weight Gross	Pounds Net	Cubic Meas. Feet
500	Cabad	No. 0 Sun	2	3	$6\frac{1}{2}$	12 doz. Box	51	26	5.4
502	Cabel	No. 1 Sun	$2\frac{1}{2}$	$3\frac{1}{2}$	$7\frac{1}{2}$	12 doz. Box	68	36	8.1
504	Cabin	No. 2 Sun	3	4	$8\frac{1}{2}$	12 doz. Box	94	44	10.7

Sun Bulb or Bulge Comet—Plain Top
For Sun Burners, Eureka, Queen Anne, etc

Number	Code Word	Description	Diam. Inches Fitting	Diam. Inches Bulb	Height Inches	Standard Package	Weight Gross	Pounds Net	Cubic Meas. Feet
19	Cabot	No. 0 Sun	2	3	$6\frac{1}{2}$	12 doz. Box	51	26	5.4
20	Cabre	No. 1 Sun	$2\frac{1}{2}$	$3\frac{1}{4}$	$7\frac{1}{2}$	12 doz. Box	68	36	8.1
20 L	Cacae	No. 1 Sun, Long 9″	$2\frac{1}{2}$	$3\frac{1}{4}$	9	12 doz. Box	78	40	9.
21	Cavaj	No. 2 Sun	3	4	$8\frac{1}{2}$	12 doz. Box	94	44	10.7
21 L	Cacia	No. 2 Sun, Long $9\frac{1}{2}$″	3	4	$9\frac{1}{2}$	12 doz. Box	100	50	10.8
21 S	Caden	No. 2 Sun, Short	3	4	$7\frac{3}{4}$	12 doz. Box	90	40	9.9
389	Cadre	No. 2 Sun, Short 5″	3	4	5	12 doz. Box	85	37	10.7
25	Cadle	No. 2 Sun, Slim for Globe	3	$3\frac{3}{8}$	$8\frac{1}{2}$	12 doz. Box	90	40	9.9
21 B	Cadie	No. 2 Sun, Oval Bulb	3	$3\frac{7}{8}$	8	12 doz. Box	94	44	10.7

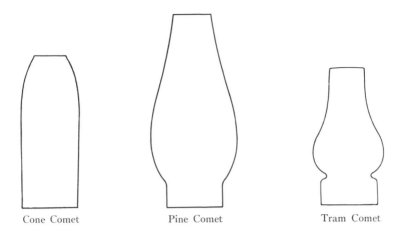

Cone Comet   Pine Comet   Tram Comet

Cone or Straight Comet

For Sun Burners, Eureka, Queen Anne, etc

Number	Code Word	Description	Diam. Inches Fitting	Height Inches	Standard Package	Weight Pounds Gross	Net	Cubic Meas. Feet
$22\frac{1}{2}$	Cadus	No. 0 Sun	2	$6\frac{1}{2}$	12 doz. Box	48	30	5.3
23	Cadot	No. 1 Sun	$2\frac{1}{2}$	$7\frac{1}{8}$	12 doz. Box	58	38	6.9
24	Cadif	No. 2 Sun	3	8	12 doz. Box	87	50	9.9

Pine Comet

For Sun Burners, Eureka, Queen Anne, etc

Number	Code Word	Description	Diam. Ins. Fit'g Bulb	Height Inches	Standard Package	Weight Lbs. Gross	Net	Cubic Meas. Feet
390	Caiop	No. 7 Pine Comet	$2\frac{1}{2}$ 4	$8\frac{1}{2}$	12 doz. Box	94	44	10.7
359	Caire	No. 10 Pine Comet	3 $4\frac{1}{2}$	9	12 doz. Box	100	50	10.8
390S	Caiva	No. 7 Pine Comet, Sand Blast	$2\frac{1}{2}$ 4	$8\frac{1}{2}$	12 doz. Box	94	44	10.7
359S	Caiso	No. 10 Pine Comet, Sand Blast	3 $4\frac{1}{2}$	9	12 doz. Box	100	50	10.8
390E	Cains	No. 7 Pine Comet, Etched	$2\frac{1}{2}$ $4\frac{1}{2}$	$8\frac{1}{2}$	12 doz. Box	112	50	10.8
359E	Caiph	No. 10 Pine Comet, Etched	3 $4\frac{5}{8}$	10	12 doz. Box	166	56	16.2

Tram Comet

For Sun Burners, Eureka, Queen Anne, etc

Number	Code Word	Description	Diameter Inches Fitting Bulb	Height Inches	Standard Package	Weight Pounds Gross	Net	Cubic Meas. Feet
386	Cagna	$\frac{3}{8}$ Tram	$2\frac{1}{16}$ 3	6	12 doz. Box	51	26	5.4
387	Cagli	$\frac{5}{8}$ Tram	$2\frac{1}{2}$ $3\frac{3}{8}$	$6\frac{1}{4}$	12 doz. Box	67	32	8.1
388	Cagmo	$\frac{7}{8}$ Tram	3 $3\frac{3}{4}$	$7\frac{1}{4}$	12 doz. Box	90	40	9.

Large Bulge, Engraved

Large Bulge, Pearl Top

Large Bulge
Etched Empire

Large Bulge, Etched Diana
Globe and Mammoth

Large Bulge—Clear
For Sun Burners, Eureka, Queen Anne, etc

Number	Code Word	Description	Diam. Inches Fitting Bulb	Height Inches	Standard Package	Weight Pounds Gross	Net	Cubic Meas. Feet
520	Calka	No. 1 Globe	$2\frac{1}{2}$ $4\frac{3}{4}$	$7\frac{3}{4}$	12 doz. Box	114	44	10.8
522	Calar	No. 2 Globe	3 5	$8\frac{1}{2}$	12 doz. Box	166	56	16.2
521	Calco	No. 1 Mammoth Globe	$2\frac{1}{2}$ $4\frac{3}{4}$	$8\frac{3}{4}$	12 doz. Box	166	56	16.2
523	Calin	No. 2 Mammoth Globe	3 $5\frac{3}{4}$	$10\frac{5}{8}$	3 doz. Box	65	18	9.0
505	Calam	No. 1 Little Giant	$2\frac{1}{2}$ 4	$7\frac{1}{2}$	12 doz. Box	103	40	9.9
506	Culry	No. 2 Little Giant	3 $4\frac{1}{2}$	$8\frac{1}{2}$	12 doz. Box	150	50	14.4

Large Bulge—Engraved and Etched
For Sun Burners, Eureka, Queen Anne, etc

Number	Code Word	Description	Diam. Inches Fitting Bulb	Height Inches	Standard Package	Weight Pounds Gross	Net	Cubic Meas. Feet
520 D	Calot	No. 1 Globe Etched, Diana	$2\frac{1}{2}$ $4\frac{3}{4}$	$7\frac{3}{4}$	12 doz. Box	114	44	10.8
522 D	Calhu	No. 2 Globe Etched, Diana	3 5	$8\frac{1}{2}$	6 doz. Box	72	28	9.0
520 E	Camar	No. 1 Globe Etched, Empire	$2\frac{1}{2}$ $4\frac{3}{4}$	$7\frac{3}{4}$	12 doz. Box	114	44	10.8
522 E	Cambe	No. 2 Globe Etched, Empire	3 5	$8\frac{1}{2}$	6 doz. Box	72	28	9.0
520 O	Camco	No. 1 Globe Etch., Owl and Star	$2\frac{1}{2}$ $4\frac{1}{4}$	$7\frac{1}{4}$	12 doz. Box	114	44	10.8
522 O	Camdu	No. 2 Globe Etch., Owl and Star	3 5	$8\frac{1}{2}$	6 doz. Box	72	28	9.0
521 D	Camel	No. 1 Mammoth Etched, Diana	$2\frac{1}{2}$ $4\frac{3}{4}$	$8\frac{3}{4}$	6 doz. Box	72	28	9.0
523 D	Camfy	No. 2 Mammoth Etched, Diana	3 $5\frac{3}{4}$	$10\frac{5}{8}$	3 doz. Box	65	18	9.0
520 Eng	Calde	No. 1 Globe Engraved	$2\frac{1}{2}$ $4\frac{3}{4}$	$7\frac{3}{4}$	6 doz. Box	50	22	6.0
522 Eng	Calex	No. 2 Globe Engraved	3 5	$8\frac{1}{2}$	6 doz. Box	72	28	9.0

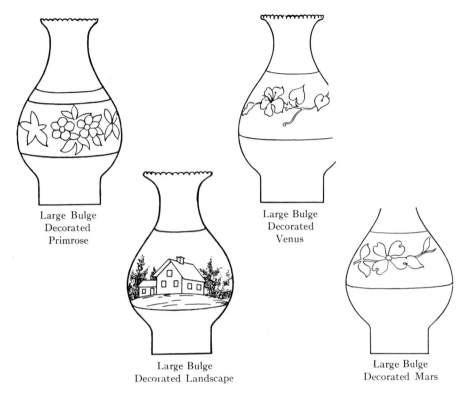

Large Bulge
Decorated
Primrose

Large Bulge
Decorated
Venus

Large Bulge
Decorated Landscape

Large Bulge
Decorated Mars

Large Bulge—Decorated

Primrose: Clear Background, Painted Flowers, Bands. Venus: Tinted Band, Painted Flowers.
Landscape: Decorated Band, Landscape. Mars: White Band, Painted Flowers

For Sun Burners, Eureka, Queen Anne, etc

Number	Code Word	Description	Diam. Inches Fitting	Bulb	Height Inches	Standard Package	Weight Pounds Gross	Net	Cubic Meas. Feet
520P	Camgi	No. 1 Globe Decorated, Primrose	$2\frac{1}{2}$	$4\frac{3}{4}$	$7\frac{3}{4}$	12 doz. Box	114	44	10.8
522P	Camha	No. 2 Globe Decorated, Primrose	3	5	$8\frac{1}{2}$	6 doz. Box	72	28	9.
520V	Camin	No. 1 Globe Decorated, Venus	$2\frac{1}{2}$	$4\frac{3}{4}$	$7\frac{3}{4}$	12 doz. Box	114	44	10.8
522V	Canal	No. 2 Globe Decorated, Venus	3	5	$8\frac{1}{2}$	6 doz. Box	72	28	9.
520L	Candy	No. 1 Globe Decorated, Landscape	$2\frac{1}{2}$	$4\frac{3}{4}$	$7\frac{3}{4}$	12 doz. Box	114	44	10.8
522L	Canon	No. 2 Globe Decorated, Landscape	3	5	$8\frac{1}{2}$	6 doz. Box	72	28	9.
520M	Canpu	No. 1 Globe Decorated, Mars	$2\frac{1}{2}$	$4\frac{3}{4}$	$7\frac{3}{4}$	12 doz. Box	114	44	10.8
522M	Canot	No. 2 Globe Decorated, Mars	3	5	$8\frac{1}{2}$	6 doz. Box	72	28	9.

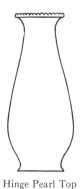

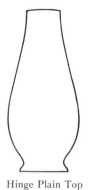

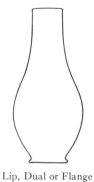

Hinge Pearl Top   Hinge Plain Top   Lip, Dual or Flange

Hinge—Pearl Top
For Sun Hinge Burners, Favorite, Excelsior, etc
(Do not confuse with Lip or Dual)

Number	Code Word	Description	Diameter Inches Fitting	Inches Bulb	Height Inches	Standard Package	Weight Gross	Pounds Net	Cubic Meas. Feet
510	Canzi	No. 0 Sun Hinge	$1\frac{7}{8}$	$2\frac{3}{4}$	6	12 doz. Box	62	24	5.4
512	Cansa	No. 1 Sun Hinge	$2\frac{3}{8}$	$3\frac{1}{4}$	$7\frac{1}{2}$	12 doz. Box	79	36	7.2
514	Canre	No. 2 Sun Hinge	$2\frac{5}{8}$	$3\frac{1}{2}$	$8\frac{1}{4}$	12 doz. Box	89	44	9.
516	Caned	No. 3 Sun Hinge	$3\frac{1}{4}$	$4\frac{1}{4}$	$9\frac{3}{8}$	3 doz. Box	40	16	5.

Hinge—Plain Top
For Sun Hinge Burners, Favorite, Excelsior, etc
(Do not confuse with Lip or Dual)

Number	Code Word	Description	Diam. Inches Fitting	Inches Bulb	Height Inches	Standard Package	Weight Gross	Pounds Net	Cubic Meas. Feet
$26\frac{1}{2}$	Caner	No. 0 Sun Hinge	$1\frac{7}{8}$	$2\frac{13}{16}$	$6\frac{3}{8}$	12 doz. Box	62	24	5.4
27	Canna	No. 1 Sun Hinge	$2\frac{3}{8}$	$3\frac{1}{4}$	$7\frac{1}{4}$	12 doz. Box	79	36	7.2
28	Canoe	No. 2 Sun Hinge	$2\frac{5}{8}$	$3\frac{3}{4}$	$8\frac{1}{4}$	12 doz. Box	89	44	9.
$28\frac{1}{2}$	Caper	No. 2 Sun Hinge, 6"	$2\frac{5}{8}$	$3\frac{1}{2}$	6	12 doz. Box	79	36	7.2
29	Cappo	No. 2 Sun Hinge, Slim	$2\frac{5}{8}$	$3\frac{1}{4}$	$8\frac{1}{4}$	12 doz. Box	89	44	9.
518	Capen	No. 3 Sun Hinge	$3\frac{1}{4}$	$4\frac{3}{8}$	10	3 doz. Box	40	16	5.
347	Chelc	Dietz Bestov Lamp	$2\frac{3}{8}$	3	6	12 doz. Box	79	36	7.2

Lip, Dual or Flange
For Railway or Ship Lamps
(Do not confuse with Hinge)

Number	Code Word	Description	Diameter Inches Fitting	Inches Bulb	Height Inches	Standard Package	Weight Gross	Pounds Net	Cubic Meas. Feet
68	Capno	No. 0 Dual	$1\frac{3}{8}$	$2\frac{1}{2}$	6	12 doz. Box	68	30	4.7
69	Capit	No. 1 Dual, 6"	$1\frac{5}{8}$	3	6	12 doz. Box	72	32	6.3
70	Capla	No. 1 Dual, 7"	$1\frac{5}{8}$	3	7	12 doz. Box	74	34	6.9
71	Capob	No. 2 Dual, 6"	$2\frac{1}{8}$	$3\frac{1}{8}$	6	12 doz. Box	90	40	8.1
72	Capra	No. 2 Dual, $6\frac{1}{4}$", Slim	$2\frac{1}{8}$	3	$6\frac{1}{4}$	12 doz. Box	90	40	8.1
73	Capsu	No. 2 Dual, $5\frac{1}{2}$"	$2\frac{1}{8}$	$3\frac{1}{4}$	$5\frac{1}{2}$	12 doz. Box	90	40	8.1
74	Capac	No. 2 Dual, 7"	$2\frac{1}{8}$	$3\frac{1}{2}$	7	12 doz. Box	94	44	8.5
75	Caput	No. 2 Dual, 7", Slim	$2\frac{1}{8}$	$3\frac{1}{4}$	7	12 doz. Box	94	44	8.5
76	Capde	No. 2 Dual, 8"	$2\frac{1}{8}$	$3\frac{5}{8}$	8	12 doz. Box	100	48	9.
77	Capmi	No. 2 Dual, 8", Slim	$2\frac{1}{8}$	3	8	12 doz. Box	96	44	8.5
78	Capgy	No. 2 Dual, 9"	$2\frac{1}{8}$	$3\frac{3}{4}$	9	12 doz. Box	113	50	9.9
79	Capzl	No. 2 Dual, 9", Slim	$2\frac{1}{8}$	$3\frac{1}{2}$	9	12 doz. Box	113	50	9.9
515	Capca	No. 3 Lip	$2\frac{3}{4}$	$4\frac{1}{4}$	10	3 doz. Box	40	16	5.

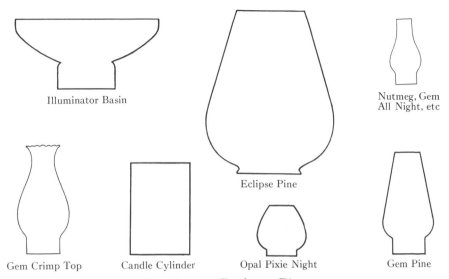

Illuminator Basin

Nutmeg, Gem
All Night, etc

Eclipse Pine

Gem Crimp Top   Candle Cylinder   Opal Pixie Night   Gem Pine

Illuminator Basin or Plate
For Sun Burners, Eureka, Queen Anne, etc

Number	Code Word	Description	Diameter Inches Fitting	Bulb	Height Inches	Standard Package	Weight Pounds Gross	Net	Cubic Meas. Feet
524	Canus	No. 1 Sun	$2\frac{1}{2}$	$7\frac{1}{4}$	$3\frac{1}{4}$	3 doz. Box	60	30	5.
526	Canto	No. 2 Sun	3	$7\frac{1}{4}$	$3\frac{1}{4}$	3 doz. Box	60	30	5.
511	Canba	No. 70	$2\frac{5}{8}$	$7\frac{1}{16}$	$3\frac{3}{16}$	3 doz. Box	60	30	5.
513	Caniv	No. 50	$2\frac{1}{16}$	$7\frac{1}{16}$	$3\frac{1}{8}$	3 doz. Box	60	30	5.

Night Lamps
Nutmeg, Gem, Opal Pixie, Candle Cylinder, etc

Number	Code Word	Description	Diameter Inches Fitting	Bulb	Height Inches	Standard Package	Weight Pounds Gross	Net	Cubic Meas. Feet
$2\frac{1}{2}$	Clove	All Night	$1\frac{7}{16}$	2	5	60 doz. Box	90	60	6.
117	Cohen	Nutmeg, Short	$1\frac{1}{4}$	$1\frac{5}{8}$	$3\frac{5}{8}$	60 doz. Box	80	45	4.5
118	Cohre	Nutmeg, Tall	$1\frac{1}{8}$	$1\frac{11}{16}$	$5\frac{1}{4}$	60 doz. Box	90	60	6.
119	Coffe	Gem	$1\frac{1}{2}$	$1\frac{7}{8}$	$4\frac{3}{4}$	60 doz. Box	90	60	6.
126	Coerr	Gem, Crimp Top	$1\frac{9}{16}$	$2\frac{3}{8}$	$5\frac{1}{16}$	60 doz. Box	95	60	7.
393	Coney	Gem, Pine, $4\frac{7}{8}''$	$1\frac{5}{8}$	$2\frac{9}{16}$	$4\frac{7}{8}$	60 doz. Box	90	60	6.
393 A	Cofin	Gem, Pine, $5\frac{5}{8}''$	$1\frac{5}{8}$	$2\frac{9}{16}$	$5\frac{5}{8}$	60 doz. Box	95	65	7.
557	Corow	Opal Pixie Night	$1\frac{5}{8}$	$2\frac{1}{8}$	$2\frac{3}{16}$	60 doz. Box	85	34	7.9
*538	Cluvi	Candle Cylinder	$2\frac{5}{8}$	$2\frac{5}{8}$	4	60 doz. Box	95	65	6.

Eclipse Pine

Number	Code Word	Description	Diameter Inches Fitting	Bulb	Height Inches	Standard Package	Weight Pounds Gross	Net	Cubic Meas. Feet
268/5	Carat	No. 5 Clear	$2\frac{1}{2}$	4	$6\frac{1}{2}$	12 doz. Box	102	40	9.9
268	Carbo	No. 7 Clear	$2\frac{3}{4}$	$5\frac{5}{8}$	$7\frac{1}{2}$	12 doz. Box	114	44	10.8
269	Carwa	No. 10 Clear	3	6	$8\frac{1}{2}$	3 doz. Box	60	18	7.
268/5S	Carta	No. 5 Sand Blast	$2\frac{1}{2}$	4	$6\frac{1}{2}$	12 doz. Box	102	40	9.9
268S	Carob	No. 7 Sand Blast	$2\frac{3}{4}$	$5\frac{5}{8}$	$7\frac{1}{2}$	12 doz. Box	114	44	10.8
269S	Cardi	No. 10 Sand Blast	3	6	$8\frac{1}{2}$	3 doz. Box	60	18	7.
268/5E	Caron	No. 5 Etched	$2\frac{1}{2}$	4	$6\frac{1}{2}$	12 doz. Box	102	40	9.9
268E	Cariz	No. 7 Etched	$2\frac{1}{4}$	$5\frac{5}{8}$	$7\frac{1}{2}$	12 doz. Box	114	44	10.8
269E	Carny	No. 10 Etched	3	6	$8\frac{1}{2}$	3 doz. Box	60	18	7.

*Cylinders of all sizes can be furnished.

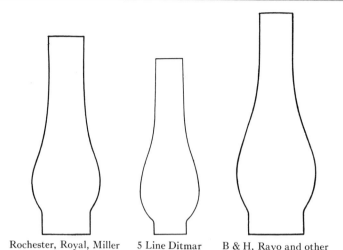

Rochester, Royal, Miller and other Central-Draft Lamps

5 Line Ditmar Little Jewel, etc

B & H, Rayo and other Central-Draft Lamps

Duplex Oval or Round

Rochester Central Draft

For Rochester, Royal, Miller, Ditmar, etc

Number	Code Word	Description	Diam. Inches Fitting	Inches Bulb	Height Inches	Standard Package	Weight Lbs. Gross	Net	Cubic Meas. Feet
4	Cella	No. 0 or Junior	$1\frac{9}{16}$	$2\frac{1}{4}$	7	12 doz. Box	52	20	5.4
6	Cecil	No. 1 8″	2	3	8	12 doz. Box	66	36	5.8
7	Cemin	No. 1 9″	2	3	9	12 doz. Box	70	40	6.2
8	Cebre	No. 2 9″	$2\frac{5}{8}$	$3\frac{5}{8}$	9	12 doz. Box	84	44	8.9
12	Cawei	No. 2 10″	$2\frac{5}{8}$	$3\frac{5}{8}$	10	12 doz. Box	88	48	9.
9	Cedar	No. 2 12″	$2\frac{5}{8}$	$3\frac{5}{8}$	12	12 doz. Box	109	66	10.
361	Cydre	No. 2 14″	$2\frac{5}{8}$	$3\frac{5}{8}$	14	12 doz. Box	168	80	13.5
362	Celan	No. 2 15″	$2\frac{5}{8}$	$3\frac{5}{8}$	15	12 doz. Box	178	90	14.
49	Celli	No. 2 10″, Slim for Globe	$2\frac{5}{8}$	$3\frac{1}{4}$	10	12 doz. Box	88	48	9.
64	Cerio	No. 2 12″, Slim for Globe	$2\frac{5}{8}$	$3\frac{1}{4}$	12	12 doz. Box	109	66	10.
363	Ceral	No. 2 14″, Slim for Globe	$2\frac{5}{8}$	$3\frac{1}{4}$	14	12 doz. Box	168	80	13.5
364	Chand	No. 2 15″, Slim for Globe	$2\frac{5}{8}$	$3\frac{1}{4}$	15	12 doz. Box	178	90	14.
10	Chapy	No. 3 or Mammoth	4	$5\frac{5}{8}$	12	2 doz. Box	35	20	4.8
26	Child	*Little Royal or Jewel	$1\frac{3}{8}$	$2\frac{1}{4}$	$7\frac{5}{8}$	12 doz. Box	52	20	5.4
396	Cholo	Ditmar 5 Line	$1\frac{5}{32}$	$2\frac{5}{8}$	$7\frac{5}{8}$	12 doz. Box	52	20	5.4

*Do not confuse with No 4 Jr or O Rochester

B & H Central Draft

For B & H Pittsburgh Rayo, etc

Number	Code Word	Description	Diameter Inches Fitting	Inches Bulb	Height Inches	Standard Package	Weight Lbs. Gross	Net	Cubic Meas. Feet
22	Cipes	No. 2 B & H, 10″	$2\frac{9}{16}$	$3\frac{1}{2}$	$10\frac{1}{8}$	12 doz. Box	99	54	9.
18	Cimes	No. 2 B & H, 12″	$2\frac{9}{16}$	$3\frac{5}{8}$	12	12 doz. Box	109	66	10.5
367	Cinia	No. 2 B & H, 14″	$2\frac{9}{16}$	$3\frac{5}{8}$	14	12 doz. Box	168	80	13.5
368	Cilly	No. 2 B & H, 15″	$2\frac{9}{16}$	$3\frac{5}{8}$	15	12 doz. Box	178	90	14.

Duplex Oval or Round

For Duplex, Oxford, etc

Number	Code Word	Description	Diameter Inches Fitting	Inches Bulb	Height Inches	Standard Package	Weight Pounds Gross	Net	Cubic Meas. Feet
14B	Cirks	Oval Bulb	$2\frac{1}{2}$	$3\frac{1}{4}$	$9\frac{1}{2}$	12 doz. Box	110	54	8.9
14	Crick	Round Bulb	$2\frac{1}{2}$	$3\frac{5}{8}$	$9\frac{1}{2}$	12 doz. Box	110	54	8.9

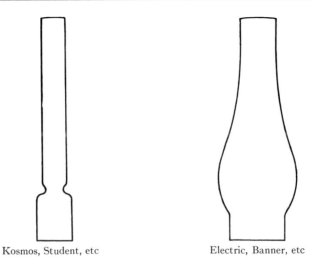

Kosmos, Student, etc   Electric, Banner, etc

Kosmos or Student
For Kosmos, Student and Other Reading Lamps

Number	Code Word	Description	Diameter Fitting Inches	Height Inches	Standard Package	Weight Pounds Gross	Net	Cubic Meas. Feet
54	Ciuti	No. 6 Line Kosmos	$1\frac{5}{16}$	$7\frac{1}{2}$	12 doz. Box	30	18	2.
56	Civil	No. 8 Line Kosmos	$1\frac{3}{8}$	9	12 doz. Box	40	22	3.
58	Claff	No. 10 Line Kosmos	$1\frac{1}{2}$	10	12 doz. Box	45	24	3.
379	Chars	No. 12 Line Kosmos	$1\frac{3}{4}$	$10\frac{3}{16}$	12 doz. Box	50	30	4.6
53A	Clors	No. 14 Line Kosmos, Short	$2\frac{1}{16}$	7	12 doz. Box	41	21	3.
53B	Clark	No. 14 Line Kosmos	$2\frac{1}{16}$	$10\frac{1}{8}$	12 doz. Box	50	30	4.6
380	Class	No. 16 Line Kosmos	$2\frac{5}{16}$	11	12 doz. Box	65	40	5.4
196M1	Clemy	Miller Student Reading Lamp	$1\frac{15}{16}$	$9\frac{1}{2}$	12 doz. Box	45	24	3.
196M5	Clira	Miller Student Reading Lamp	$1\frac{15}{16}$	$8\frac{1}{2}$	12 doz. Box	43	22	3.
354	Clipe	Toy (Student)	$1\frac{3}{16}$	$3\frac{7}{16}$	60 doz. Box	80	45	5.
50	Cloyd	No. 1 Student, $10\frac{1}{2}''$	$1\frac{15}{16}$	$10\frac{1}{2}$	12 doz. Box	50	30	4.6
51	Claud	No. 1 Student, $9\frac{1}{2}''$	$1\frac{15}{16}$	$9\frac{1}{2}$	12 doz. Box	50	30	4.6
48	Clune	No. 2 Student	$1\frac{3}{4}$	$10\frac{1}{2}$	12 doz. Box	50	30	4.6
52	Clubz	No. 9 or Mammoth Student	$2\frac{1}{4}$	11	12 doz. Box	65	40	5.4
376	Clupy	Queens Reading, 14 Line Student	$1\frac{7}{8}$	$10\frac{1}{4}$	12 doz. Box	50	30	4.6
114	Clute	Bristol Student	$2\frac{1}{16}$	10	12 doz. Box	65	40	5.4

Electric or Banner
For Climax, Queen Anne, etc

Number	Code Word	Description	Diam. Inches Fitting	Bulb	Height Inches	Standard Package	Weight Pounds Gross	Net	Cubic Meas. Feet
41	Chime	No. 1	$2\frac{1}{2}$	$3\frac{1}{2}$	9	12 doz. Box	77	40	9.
40	Chilo	No. 2 10''	3	4	10	12 doz. Box	99	56	10.8
357	China	No. 2 12''	3	4	12	12 doz. Box	120	70	12.6
63	Chiga	No. 2 10'', Slim Straight Sides for Globe	3	$3\frac{3}{8}$	10	12 doz. Box	99	56	9.
356	Chain	No. 2 12'', Slim Straight Sides for Globe	3	$3\frac{3}{8}$	12	12 doz. Box	109	66	10.5
65	Chrew	No. 2 10'', Slim Regular Shape for Globe	3	$3\frac{3}{8}$	10	12 doz. Box	99	56	9.
358	Champ	No. 2 12'', Slim Regular Shape for Globe	3	$3\frac{3}{8}$	12	12 doz. Box	109	66	10.5

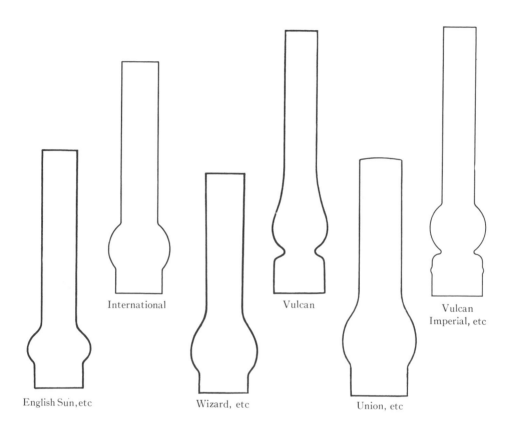

International

Vulcan

Vulcan
Imperial, etc

English Sun, etc

Wizard, etc

Union, etc

Central Draft Lamps
Wizard, English Sun, Union, Vulcan and Wonder

Number	Code Word	Description	Diam. Inches Fitting	Bulb	Height Inches	Standard Package	Weight Pounds Gross	Net	Cubic Meas. Feet
381	Cruse	15 Line Wizard, etc.	$1\frac{7}{8}$	$2\frac{1}{4}$	$10\frac{1}{4}$	24 doz. Box	98	60	7.2
365	Citza	15 Line Wizard, Short	$1\frac{7}{8}$	$2\frac{1}{4}$	9	24 doz. Box	98	60	7.2
385	Czaja	20 Line English Sun, etc.	$2\frac{1}{2}$	$3\frac{3}{16}$	$10\frac{3}{4}$	12 doz. Box	99	54	7.6
124	Czerm	No. 1 Union, etc.	$2\frac{1}{16}$	$3\frac{5}{16}$	$9\frac{1}{2}$	24 doz. Box	130	80	10.8
125	Cytol	No. 2 Union, etc.	$2\frac{5}{8}$	$3\frac{5}{8}$	$10\frac{3}{4}$	12 doz. Box	99	54	7.6
127	Cyria	16 Line Vulcan, Imperial, etc.	$2\frac{1}{4}$	$2\frac{1}{2}$	$11\frac{1}{2}$	12 doz. Box	110	60	9.
128	Cysta	Vulcan Ribbed Heel	$2\frac{1}{4}$	$2\frac{5}{8}$	$11\frac{3}{4}$	12 doz. Box	110	60	9.
113	Czine	18 Line Vulcan, Imperial, etc.	$2\frac{7}{16}$	$2\frac{5}{8}$	12	12 doz. Box	110	60	9.
110	Cyral	Vulcan Ribbed Heel	$2\frac{13}{16}$	$2\frac{15}{16}$	12	12 doz. Box	110	60	9.
17	Conti	18 Line Odin Wonder, etc.	$2\frac{7}{16}$	$3\frac{1}{4}$	$10\frac{1}{4}$	12 doz. Box	99	54	7.6
397	Covix	16 Line International	$2\frac{1}{16}$	$2\frac{11}{16}$	10	12 doz. Box	108	56	9.

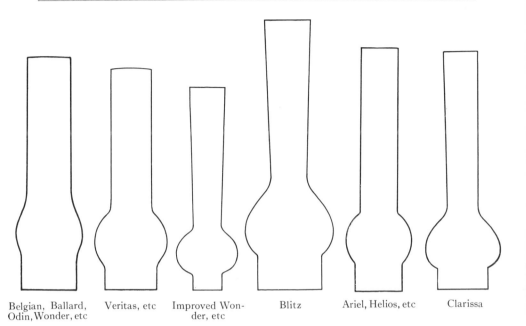

Belgian, Ballard, Odin, Wonder, etc   Veritas, etc   Improved Wonder, etc   Blitz   Ariel, Helios, etc   Clarissa

Central Draft Lamps
Belge, Veritas, Ariel, Improved Wonder, Blitz and Clarissa

Number	Code Word	Description	Diameter Fitting	Inches Bulb	Height Inches	Standard Package	Weight Gross	Pounds Net	Cubic Meas. Feet
30	Conel	No. 2 Belgian, 14 Line	$1\frac{7}{8}$	$2\frac{1}{4}$	9	24 doz. Box	98	60	7.2
32	Costs	No. 1 Belgian, 20 Line	$2\frac{1}{2}$	3	$10\frac{1}{4}$	12 doz. Box	99	54	8.
57	Cupid	No. 1 Belgian, 12″ long	$2\frac{1}{2}$	3	12	12 doz. Box	110	60	9.
369	Cotil	No. 1 Belgian, 14″ long	$2\frac{1}{2}$	3	14	12 doz. Box	168	80	13.5
370	Cotta	No. 1 Belgian, 15″ long	$2\frac{1}{2}$	3	15	12 doz. Box	178	90	14.
371	Cosmo	No. 1 Belgian, 16″ long	$2\frac{1}{2}$	3	16	12 doz. Box	188	100	14.4
36	Cossa	No. 00 Belgian, 30 Line	3	$3\frac{1}{2}$	$12\frac{1}{8}$	12 doz. Box	143	70	10.1
43	Craig	No. 00 Belgian, 9″ long	3	$3\frac{1}{2}$	9	12 doz. Box	110	60	9.
34	Craft	No. 0 Belgian, 25 Line Wonder	$2\frac{5}{8}$	3	$11\frac{1}{2}$	12 doz. Box	110	60	9.
33	Crags	Ballard	$2\frac{5}{8}$	3	10	12 doz. Box	99	54	7.6
129	Chase	20 Line Veritas	$2\frac{1}{2}$	$3\frac{3}{8}$	$10\frac{1}{2}$	12 doz. Box	99	54	7.6
37	Craem	30 Line Veritas	$3\frac{1}{16}$	$3\frac{7}{8}$	$12\frac{7}{16}$	12 doz. Box	175	70	14.2
384	Crabs	60 Line Veritas	$4\frac{1}{4}$	6	12	2 doz. Box	35	20	4.8
375	Crush	16 Line Ariel, Helios, etc.	$2\frac{1}{8}$	3	$10\frac{3}{8}$	12 doz. Box	99	54	7.6
373	Crobj	10 Line Improved Wonder, etc.	$1\frac{1}{2}$	$2\frac{1}{2}$	$8\frac{3}{4}$	24 doz. Box	99	60	7.2
964	Crops	30 Line Blitz, etc.	$2\frac{15}{16}$	4	12	12 doz. Box	175	70	10.1
374	Culpe	20 Line Clarissa, etc.	$2\frac{1}{2}$	3	$10\frac{3}{4}$	12 doz. Box	99	54	7.6

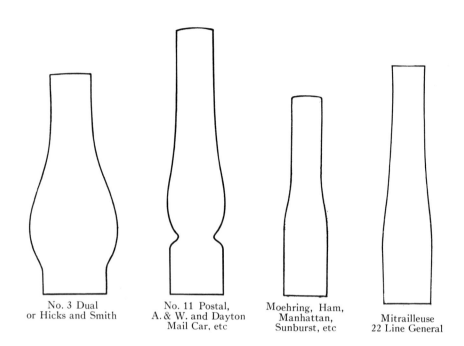

| No. 3 Dual or Hicks and Smith | No. 11 Postal, A. & W. and Dayton Mail Car, etc | Moehring, Ham, Manhattan, Sunburst, etc | Mitrailleuse 22 Line General |

*Railway Headlight, Coach Lamps, etc

Number	Code Word	Description	Diameter Inches Fitting	Diameter Inches Bulb	Height Inches	Standard Package	Weight Pounds Gross	Weight Pounds Net	Cubic Meas. Feet
16	Coker	No. 3 Dual or Hicks & Smith	$2\frac{1}{2}$	$3\frac{5}{8}$	$10\frac{1}{8}$	12 doz. Box	90	52	9.
44	Cobeb	No. 11 Postal	$2\frac{1}{2}$	$2\frac{3}{4}$	12	12 doz. Box	110	60	9.
86	Coiro	Manhattan Lard Oil	$2\frac{3}{8}$	$2\frac{3}{8}$	12	12 doz. Box	110	62	9.
87	Cohoe	Ham Motor Headlight	$1\frac{15}{16}$	$1\frac{15}{16}$	10	12 doz. Box	88	30	5.4
88	Colon	No. 3 Moehring	2	2	$10\frac{1}{2}$	12 doz. Box	94	44	5.4
84	Colar	No. 3 Moehring, 6″	2	2	6	12 doz. Box	58	20	3.6
85	Cowry	No. 3 Moehring, $5\frac{1}{2}$″	2	2	$5\frac{1}{2}$	12 doz. Box	58	20	3.6
89	Culak	No. 3 Moehring, 9″	2	2	9	12 doz. Box	90	40	5.4
355	Cudmo	Sunburst	$2\frac{1}{4}$	$2\frac{1}{4}$	12	12 doz. Box	110	60	9.
115	Clays	Mitrailleuse	$2\frac{1}{8}$	$2\frac{1}{8}$	$10\frac{1}{2}$	12 doz. Box	65	40	9.
116	Conew	22 Line General	$2\frac{1}{16}$	$2\frac{11}{16}$	10	12 doz. Box	110	54	9.

*A special catalogue covering railway lamp glasses, lantern globes, lenses, shades, etc, will be furnished on request.

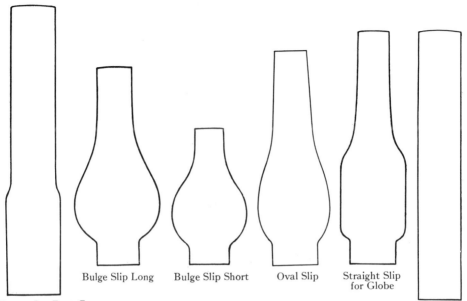

Bulge Slip Long   Bulge Slip Short   Oval Slip   Straight Slip for Globe

Kronos, Sun Dart, Canchester and other Kerosene Mantle Lamps

Wonder Kerosene Mantle Lamp, etc

Bulge Slip
For ¾ and 1 Inch Slip Burners

Number	Code Word	Description	Diameter Inches Fitting	Diameter Inches Bulb	Height Inches	Standard Package	Weight Pounds Gross	Weight Pounds Net	Cubic Meas. Feet
190	Cusle	No. 8 Short	$1\frac{3}{4}$	$2\frac{3}{4}$	6	12 doz. Box	50	26	5.5
193	Curts	No. 10 Short	$2\frac{1}{16}$	4	7	12 doz. Box	60	35	8.5
197	Custi	No. 8 Long	$1\frac{3}{4}$	$3\frac{3}{4}$	9	12 doz. Box	78	40	9.
194	Curep	No. 10 Long	$2\frac{1}{16}$	4	9	12 doz. Box	84	44	9.
394	Cuort	No. 8 Oval Slip	$1\frac{3}{4}$	$3\frac{5}{16}$	9	12 doz. Box	105	45	7.5
13 B	Cualo	No. 10 Oval Slip	$2\frac{1}{16}$	3	9	12 doz. Box	105	45	7.5

Straight Slip for Globe
For ¾ and 1 Inch Slip Burners

Number	Code Word	Description	Diameter Inches Fitting	Diameter Inches Bulb	Height Inches	Standard Package	Weight Pounds Gross	Weight Pounds Net	Cubic Meas. Feet
198	Cuntz	No. 8	$1\frac{3}{4}$	$2\frac{1}{2}$	10	12 doz. Box	102	42	7.6
195	Cusac	No. 10	$2\frac{1}{16}$	3	$10\frac{1}{2}$	12 doz. Box	108	48	7.9
392	Curry	No. 8 Short	$1\frac{3}{4}$	$2\frac{1}{2}$	$7\frac{7}{8}$	12 doz. Box	69	36	5.8
391	Cuick	No. 10 Short	$2\frac{1}{16}$	3	$7\frac{3}{4}$	12 doz. Box	75	42	6.1

Kerosene Mantle Lamps

Number	Code Word	Description	Diam. Ins. Fitting	Height Inches	Standard Package	Weight Pounds Gross	Weight Pounds Net	Cubic Meas. Feet
188	Cemps	Wonder Lamp, etc.	$2\frac{1}{8}$	12	12 doz. Box	99	54	7.6
382	Cynop	Kronos, etc.	$2\frac{7}{8}$	13	12 doz. Box	110	60	9.
383	Cytre	Sun Dart, etc.	$2\frac{1}{2}$	13	12 doz. Box	110	60	9.
1050	Centr	Canchester, etc.	2	$12\frac{3}{4}$	12 doz. Box	110	60	9.

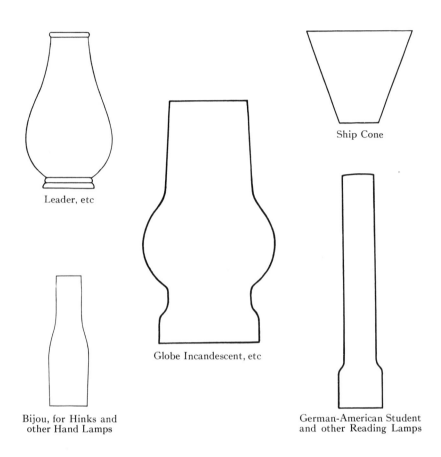

Leader, etc

Ship Cone

Globe Incandescent, etc

Bijou, for Hinks and
other Hand Lamps

German-American Student
and other Reading Lamps

Globe Incandescent and Miscellaneous Chimneys

Number	Code Word	Description	Diam. Inches Fitting	Bulb	Height Inches	Standard Package	Weight Gross	Pounds Net	Cubic Meas. Feet
66	Czero	No. 2 Globe, Incandescent	$4\frac{1}{2}$	6	11	2 doz. Box	35	20	4.8
1	Cepio	Leader	$2\frac{3}{8}$	4	7	12 doz. Box	110	60	7.2
2	Cinga	Leader	$2\frac{3}{4}$	$4\frac{1}{2}$	8	12 doz. Box	138	80	9.0
517	Cubol	Ship Cone	$1\frac{7}{8}$	5	$4\frac{1}{4}$	24 doz. Box	130	80	9.0
191	Chair	Hinks or Bijou Hand Lamp	$1\frac{3}{4}$		6	24 doz. Box	66	36	3.8
61	Cluch	German American Student	$2\frac{1}{16}$		$10\frac{1}{2}$	12 doz. Box	65	40	5.7

Fostoria Glass Co., 1906

The Fostoria Glass Co. was founded in Fostoria, Ohio, in 1887. The site was chosen because of the availability of cheap fuel from a recently opened natural gas field. The gas field proved short-lived and in 1891 Fostoria moved to Moundsville, W. Va., where it is still in operation.

Fostoria's first product was pressed ware, most of which was supplied to metal-working companies or "mounters" who mounted the articles in silver, nickel or brass frames. About 1897 Fostoria added a line of oil lamps, ranging from tiny night and fairy lamps to large vase lamps, with stress on the latter. These featured brightly colored naturalistic floral decoration. All the plates of lamps from Fostoria's 1906 catalog are reproduced in the following pages. A few pages from the catalog, devoted exclusively to vases, have been omitted.

By the time this catalog was issued, the day of the elaborate oil lamp was almost at an end. As electricity became widely available, Fostoria shifted its production to other handmolded items, including dresser sets and table sets featuring tumblers, spoon holders, sugars and creamers, and upright celery holders. Early in the century Fostoria began manufacturing fine handblown stemware for the hotel and restaurant market. As the demand for fine crystal in public establishments decreased, Fostoria shifted its attention to the domestic market.

Today Fostoria is the largest American producer of fine blown and handmolded table glassware and decorative accessories. The latter include such items as bowls, candlesticks, vases, ash trays, and figures. A few patterns are made in colored glass. An extensive range of milk glass and some "ebony" are also made. Much Fostoria glass features hand cutting, acid etching and fired-on gold and platinum patterns.

Fine Decorated Lamps

Season
1906 - 07

Fostoria Glass Co
MOUNDSVILLE, W. VA.

SATIN FINISH—GILT TRIMMINGS

No. 315 Lamp
With 9½ in. Globe.
Height 23½ in.   Crystal Glass
etched outside

No. 284 Lamp
With 10 in. Globe.
Height 23 in.   Crystal Glass.
etched outside.

NOTE: For descriptive matter see Decorated Lamp Price List.

MARY LAMP
Blue etched.

MARY LAMP,
Crystal etched.

NOTE: For descriptive matter see Decorated Lamp Price List.

ALL LAMPS FURNISHED IN TWO DECORATIONS
ONLY ONE DECORATION SHOWN

IVAN
Height 15 in.
Shade 7 in. Dec. A

IVAN
Dec. B. Same Dec.
Green tinted

NEIL
Height 15 in.
Shade 7 in. Dec. B

NEIL
Dec. A. Rose
Orange tinted.

OGDEN
Height 18 in.
Shade 7 in.   Dec. Ь

OGDEN
Height 18 in.
Globe 7½ in.   Dec. A

ALL LAMPS FURNISHED IN TWO DECORATIONS

DOVER
Height 18 in.
Globe 8 in. Dec. A

DOVER
Dec. B. Green tints

RHEA
Height 17 in.
Globe 8 in. Dec. A

RHEA
Dec. B. Dahlia
Red and Orange tint

LOUIS
Height 17 in.
Shade 8½ in. Dec. B

LOUIS
Height 17½ in.
Globe 8 in. Dec. A.

134

COLON
Height 19 in.
Shade 10 in. Dec. A

COLON
Height 20 in.
Globe 9 in. Dec. B

ALL LAMPS FURNISHED IN TWO DECORATIONS

SELMA
Height 19½ in.
Globe 9 in. Dec. A.

SELMA
Dec. B. Poppies
Brown and Yellow tinted

ALVIN
Height 22 in.
Globe 9 in. Dec. B

ALVIN
Dec. A, Xmas Flower
Pink and Yellow tinted

WALDO
Height 20½ in.
Shade 10 in. Dec. B

WALDO
Height 22½ in.
Globe 9 in. Dec. A

KIRBY
Height 18½ in.
Globe 8 in.   Dec. A

SEINE
Height 25½ in.
Globe 10 in.   Dec. A

SEINE
Dec. B.   Same as above
Blue tinted

ALL LAMPS FURNISHED IN TWO DECORATIONS

ELSIE
Height 23 in.
Globe 9 in.   Dec. B

ELSIE
Dec. A. Wild Rose
Brown tinted

MILAN
Height 23 in.
Globe 9 in.   Dec. A

MILAN
Dec. B. Wild Rose
Apple Green tint

ALL LAMPS FURNISHED IN TWO DECORATIONS

HARLAN
Height 24 in.
Globe 10 in. Dec. B.

HARLAN
Dec. A. Roses
Pink tinted

TACOMA
Height 23 in.
Globe 10 in. Dec. A

TACOMA
Dec. B. Daisies
Buff tint

140

ALL LAMPS FURNISHED IN TWO DECORATIONS

CONCORD
Height 26 in.
Globe 10 in. Dec. B

CONCORD
Dec. A. Tulip
Pink and Green tint

LOPEZ
Height 24½ in.
Globe 10 in.   Dec. B

LOPEZ
Dec. A. Yellow Roses
Brown and Pink tints

141

ALL LAMPS FURNISHED IN TWO DECORATIONS

WINTON
Height 25½ in.
Globe 10 in. Dec. A

WINTON
Dec. B. Poppies
Light Brown tint

SITKA
Height 26 in.
Globe 10 in. Dec. B.

SITKA
Dec. A. Orchid
Ruby tint

ALL LAMPS FURNISHED IN TWO DECORATIONS

IDAHO
Height 26 in.
Globe 10 in. Dec. A

IDAHO
Dec. B. Azalea
Apple Green tint

SATURN
Height 22½ in.
Globe 10 in. Dec. B

SATURN
Dec. A. Anemone
Ruby and Pink tint

143

ALL LAMPS FURNISHED IN TWO DECORATIONS

NICHOLAS
Height 28½ in.
Globe 11 in. Dec. B

NICHOLAS
Dec. A. Poppies
Brown and Green tints

ELLIOTT
Height 27½ in.
Globe 11 in. Dec. B

ELLIOTT
Dec. A. Poppies
Variegated tints

144

ALL LAMPS FURNISHED IN TWO DECORATIONS

LOWELL
Height 27½ in.
Globe 11 in.   Dec. A

LOWELL
Dec. B. Poppies
Brown and Green tints

STANLEY
Height 26 in.
Globe 11 in.   Dec. B

STANLEY
Dec. A. Roses
Pink and Ivory tints

OREGON
Height 28 in.
Globe 11 in. Dec. A

OREGON
Dec. B. Roses
Brown and Green tints

NEWARK
Height 29 in.
Globe 11 in. Dec. B

NEWARK
Dec. A. Poppies
Ruby tinted

AUGUSTA
Height 29 in.
Globe 11 in. Dec. B

AUGUSTA
Dec. A. Carnations
Pink and Ivory tints

VICTORIA
Height 25½ in.
Globe 11 in. Dec. A

VICTORIA
Dec. B. Dogs, etc.
Green tinted

ALL LAMPS FURNISHED IN TWO DECORATIONS

GENOA
Height 26 in.
Globe 12 in. Dec. B

GENOA
Dec. A. Wild Rose
Pink and Green tints

ALBANY
Height 30½ in.
Globe 12 in. Dec. B

ALBANY
Dec. A. Pansies
Pink and Ivory tints

148

ALL LAMPS FURNISHED IN TWO DECORATIONS

VENDOME
Height 32 in.
Globe 12 in. Dec. B

VENDOME
Dec. A. Roses and Snowballs
Ivory tinted

IMPERIAL
Height 31½ in.
Globe 12 in. Dec. A

IMPERIAL
Dec. B. Anemone
Ruby and Green tints

PREMIER
Height 32½ in.
Globe 12 in. Dec. A

PREMIER
Height 32½ in.
Globe 12 in. Dec. B

MISCELLANEOUS GOODS

Indian Pin Tray
Opal Dec.

Clover
Night Lamp
Ruby Cold
Stain

Rose Night Lamp

Pansy Night Lamp

Dresden Globes, 9, 10 and 11 in. sizes

SOLID BLUE GLASS
NOT ETCHED

No. 190. Lamp
With 7 in. Shade
Height 15 in.

No. 220. Lamp
With 7½ in. Globe
Height 17 in.

SOLID BLUE GLASS
ETCHED OUTSIDE

No. 315 Lamp
With 9½ in. Globe.
Height 23½ in.

No. 284
With 10 in. Globe.
Height 23 in.

153

MISCELLANEOUS

SOLID BLUE
GLASS

NOT
ETCHED

No. 1481 Pin Tray.

No. 19
Night Lamp.

No. 1025
Shaker N. T.

No. 1487
Indian Pin Tray

No. 1112 Night Lamp.

No. 1481 Comb and Brush Tray.

No. 1481 Hair Pin Box.

No. 1481 Puff Box.

No. 1481 Bottle.

154

No. 1176 Syrup, Opal dec.

No. 1059 Syrup
Opal Dec.

No. 1175 Syrup.
Opal Dec.

Household Sewing Lamp.
Crystal Glass, Plain
Etched Chimney.

"QUEEN" LAMP ASSORTMENT
OPAL GLASS—PLASTER COLLARS

HAND PAINTED DECORATIONS
COLD COLORS

No. 212	No. 212	No. 212.
O Lamp, Height 16 in.	B Lamp, Height 17½ in.	D Lamp, Height 19½ in.